She Died Young

BRENDA FRICKER
She Died Young

A Life in Fragments

An Apollo Book

MIX
Paper | Supporting
responsible forestry
FSC
www.fsc.org
FSC® C013604

Bloomsbury Publishing Plc
50 Bedford Square, London, WC1B 3DP, UK
Bloomsbury Publishing Ireland Limited,
29 Earlsfort Terrace, Dublin 2, D02 AY28, Ireland

HEAD OF ZEUS LTD
5–8 Hardwick Street
London EC1R 4RG

To find out more about our authors and books
visit www.headofzeus.com

For product safety related questions contact productsafety@bloomsbury.com

To Liz Duffy

Contents

FRICKER – February 17, 1945,
at Wentworth Nursing Home, to Bina, wife of
Desmond F. Fricker, 34 Annaville Park, Dundrum,
a daughter (Brenda).

Births, Marriages and Deaths. Irish Times, 10 March, 1945.

Brenda's parents Bina and Des with her sister Gránia,
aged about two weeks.

Sometimes I Falter

Sometimes I falter. I don't know who I am.

This leaves me open to attack. That's when the depression sneaks in.

I write these words that you're now reading. I feel obliged to inform or entertain you, to tell you about my battles with the human condition, about being young, about being old.

But I'm blank.

Do you falter?

Kerry

The arrival of the Dublin gang caused consternation in the front yard of the Kerry house. My Auntie Nora (my mother Bina's only sister), Uncle Ritchie, seven country cousins, Bina, Des, Gránia and me, were a big crowd in the small courtyard of a small farmhouse in a tiny village, Gneeveguilla, in the beautiful kingdom of Kerry. Bina was a teacher. She had plenty of time in the summer to bring us down to Kerry. Des was a journalist for the *Irish Times*. He was always busy, busy, busy, but he found time for this.

Bina, Des, and Gránia would stagger over the yard, bruised and exhausted from the seven-hour journey, hugging and kissing each other loudly and happily. It was one of the few times I saw my parents happy together in a way that didn't make me suspicious.

I always hung back a bit. Leaning on the hot car. Watching.

I needed to do my private arrival ritual before joining the family in this rare state of happiness. I would bend over and, with my city-white hands, unbuckle my clean white city sandals, rip off my ironed white socks from my clean city feet, and push those feet down hard again and again until I could feel the dirty Kerry soil soaking through the soles of my feet and into my heart.

I would gasp at the strength of the feeling that flushed through me, which always told me I was safe. The freedom to be dirty. In Dublin, my mother would tell me twenty times a day or more to wash my hands, wash my face, wash my knees. If there was no water, she'd spit on her fingers and rub it on my face. It was disgusting. In Kerry, I could be dirty. To be dirty – to be filthy dirty – was all I wanted from life.

To jump into the car in Dublin and jump out of it in Kerry gave me more happiness than I could bear. It was as if my body changed with that first touch of Kerry ground. I became a different child. To see Nonee standing there, her arms outstretched, waiting to hold me tight and say words of warmth and welcome that made my heart dance. I would run straight to her, throwing my arms around her fat legs, pushing my face into her fat belly, into her flowery wrap-around apron, smelling of bread, grass, cattle, sweat. I held so tight and smelled so deep that I was drunk with happiness. Knowing this, she would cradle my head in her hands, wiggle her nose against mine, and say, 'You're welcome, welcome, welcome.'

'They're all laid out in boxes. Go up and take what you want. Oh, and your favourites are sitting under the windowsill.'

On hearing those words, I would run across the yard, into the house, up the stairs and turn left into the front bedroom and there they were: five or six large cardboard boxes filled with all sorts of clothes. The boxes had old cardigans, pyjamas, dresses, knickers, shirts: anything you could possibly need.

Changing my clothes in Kerry was part of my secret ritual. It had a profound effect on me. I would become aware of the room around me, its walls keeping me safe, as I ripped off whatever silly, frilly dress and shiny leather shoes Bina had dressed me up in for the trip from Dublin. All you had to do was find something that fitted you. It didn't really matter what you wore in Kerry. It was so easy, here, to get dressed in five minutes, smiling from ear to ear as I picked a shirt, a skirt, and socks, and put them on like a nun putting on her garb.

At this point, I would stop. Turn my head towards the window. I would cast my eyes down beneath the window and there *they* were, exactly where I had left them one year ago. I felt utter contentment as I reached out to touch them.

My wellingtons.

All mine, no sharing. The outside of each boot was unwashed. All the dried dirt and muck. The sweet smell of cattle, the warm smell of pigs, had been waiting there all year for my return.

Nonee had asked me once or twice did I want them washed. I screeched in horror, no, no, no. 'I love the way they smell. I love them being dirty.' The dirt proved that I had done some proper farm work and I loved the muck.

Nonee understood this completely, so she never moved my wellingtons from that spot. When I was in Dublin, it gave me comfort to know that they were there, and Auntie Nonee knew that.

I could not handle this respect, this kindness. I would burst into a flood of happy tears, fling my arms around her waist and push my face against her tummy again. I would listen to the music in her voice as she said lovingly, 'It's all right, Brenda. Everything is fine. There is no danger here. You're safe here.'

She knew the wellingtons were central to everything in my transformation from Dublin jackeen to country kid, changing my life into a thing of delight. She completely understood that and protected it for me.

The joy I got from wearing the wellingtons is hard to explain. They made me feel safe. They made me feel strong. They made it possible to feel that I was *me* – the child who lived in Kerry. Was I worshipping here? Probably. No word I choose is good enough to describe that transformation, from

Brenda's Aunt Nonee.

an uptight, nervous child into an observant, thoughtful, curious, happy little girl.

I would stand and stare at them. Then I would pick them up so carefully, so slowly, as if they were made of gossamer. Touching them again sent shivers down my spine. I would lift my right leg and then, holding both sides in my city-clean hands, I would push down hard and, in one swift movement, experience a happiness that almost made me scream. As I pushed my left foot down the full length of that other boot, there was now magic in my life. I was okay now. I was no longer afraid. I was a proper, true, legitimate Kerry girl crying to God, 'Now I'm me! No sins in me here; no lies; no cover-ups.'

Auntie Nonee was a large, comfortable woman, pale-skinned from slaving indoors to keep her small farm and family turning over. She carried her smile with her and, when she was pleased with you, you would hear the softest laugh

5

behind the smile. I adored her and everything about her, especially the false teeth, which she had had since she was twenty. When she spoke, it was like castanets fighting inside her mouth and, although I rudely laughed out loud at that, she took it all with good humour, never once chastising me. She only wore them on special occasions, like when I came. She smiled at me now, showing them off, reminding me again that my arrival from Dublin to stay with her for the summer months would be the happiest time of the whole year for me. She'd gently curve her hand around my head. She'd pull my arms around her legs. I'd cling to her as tightly as I could, pushing my face into her dirty apron to breathe in the smells I had missed so much. The smell of the baking bread she'd made to welcome us made me feel a little drunk with happiness. I could hardly bear it.

Within hours of landing, I was given things to do – this was a proper small farm – like going to the well. The well she used was a three-mile bike ride up the road. I would turn at the fourth boreen and there was a well full of clear, clean water. I managed to get onto the huge old bike while my cousin Deirdre hung two buckets on it, one on each handlebar. I had a few false starts, and everyone around me laughed. The old man from across the road held the bike, coming close to me so that I could see, behind his unwashed face, a smile to break my heart. He leaned across to push me off and there it was again … the smell of tweed, old tweed. Dirty tweed. It always made me dizzy with love. For what? My father, probably.

Nostrils flaring, I cycled off. I passed Bina and Des, still unpacking in the yard, and pedalled off down the road, down beyond, where I entered into the Kerry air: not the absence of sound but the presence of silence. Once I knew that I was past the bend, out of sight and sound, about a hundred yards on, I stepped off, leaning my bike and buckets against the ditch. I climbed over the stone wall. Then I would lie there on the grass among the buttercups and daisies and spread my arms out like Jesus on the cross. I was listening and drinking in these overpowering feelings. The world was mine: the world was safe here and I consciously cherished it. I cried from happiness again: the same fat tears I cried from fear. I felt complete. I was completely safe. I smiled down at my wellingtons. I lifted my legs up in the air and danced them against the summer clouds, feeling so much at one with it all, so much a part of life. I burst out laughing when I waved up to the clouds and they waved back. My contentment was physical and I thanked God for giving me this feeling every year.

There was no rush in Kerry, so I dawdled along on the creaking old bike, loving it, myself, Nonee and the world. I could taste the happiness as I rode along past the fields I knew so well, the fields I would soon be working in, helping farmers to tend their farms.

On my daily adventures, I would wander into the farmers' yards and, without hesitation, they would recruit me as a helper in whatever was going on that day. Children were always part of the running of the farm. Paid help was expensive, so an extra pair of hands, no matter how small, was always welcome.

For years I didn't know that people used to smile and laugh at my obvious delight at putting on my boots and morphing from a troubled urban kid into a happy rural child. They would roar laughing behind their hands as I walked behind the farmers, trying to imitate their stride. My boots were a little too big for me so I had to drag them along, which delighted me, as it added authenticity to my outrageous mimicry. The farmers' walk was my favourite. Now I was in; I could feel it. I was allowed to talk and walk like the farmers. Little did they know that I was walking on air because I was no longer an imprisoned doll.

Nonee had seven children; there had once been nine: she had had two sets of twins, and one of each had died. Now she had Gránia and me too, in a home with no running water, no electricity and no bathroom. There were big green fields to do your number ones and number twos in and lots of dock leaves there for you to wipe your arse with. I listened to everything she said, and from the moment I arrived, I would unashamedly imitate her accent, which was a source of real delight to her. I loved living with her, living in her house, being her niece and part of the family.

Water was liquid gold, as we had to travel those miles to get it, and in Kerry it was treated with the deepest respect. I loved going to the well. We usually went in twos and threes but sometimes I went alone. We walked or cycled the distance, banging our empty buckets together and calling out wild music of our own: nonsense sounds, happy noises that filled the air. We'd arrive at the small well and lie flat on our bellies to give us extra reach down to the fresh water. We'd lean over, scoop the buckets until they were full, and then scoop some more with a small can until our buckets were overflowing. Carrying full buckets back along that road was hard work and hard fun. Whoever had the bike would put a bucket over each handlebar and perform a feat of balance worthy of a circus act, aiming to have at least half the water left in each bucket when we got home.

In the house, we poured the water into jugs and bowls and left the rest under the kitchen table. This water was all Nonee had to clean, cook, drink, wash ourselves and our clothes in, and also water the animals. This, of course, suited me completely. I wouldn't have to wash myself morning, noon and night, with Bina shouting, 'Behind your ears!' and 'Between your toes!' Proper washing happened only on a Saturday night, when every inch of your body was scrubbed red-raw, cleansed to receive the Blessed Host on Sunday morning.

There were no rules, just a natural shape to time. This was measured by day and night, dark and light. The days moved smoothly and quietly along, so completely different from the jarred and jagged sounds of the city.

We slept in bundles – seven cousins, Gránia and me – the nine of us in two beds, a double and a single. Night had no time, as we'd sing songs and have pillow fights. We would tell stories to each other until, exhausted, we'd collapse and pull worn old blankets, old towels, anything we could find, over our tired little bodies. And we'd sleep deeply in a pile of entangled limbs.

Sometimes, when I looked at Nonee and thought of how much I loved her, I could not contain myself. I would fly across the room and fling my arms around her legs, pushing my face into her apron. I would cry and cry and tell her how much I loved her. Sometimes, in a panic, I would kiss her gnarled fingers and beg her not to die.

'Never, ever die!' I would plead.

She would sit down on the nearest chair and put her arms around my troubled body, saying quietly how she loved me like she loved her own children. She would rock me back and forth in a smooth and soothing rhythm until my heart was still again. Then she would sit me up and bounce me on her knee, wiping tears and snots away with her dirty apron.

The feeling of being loved was always new to me. Why did my mother and father not do things like that with me? Why did I never feel from them the kind of love I got from Nonee? Why did they never give me anything as beautiful and valuable and simple as a hug?

Without those deliriously happy holidays in Kerry, I have no idea what I would be now.

The darkness in my mind was beginning to make itself known to me, but it never came to Kerry.

Kerry never let it in.

Horse Betty

Isuddenly woke up. I had fallen into a summer snooze, and dusk was close. The unwritten rule was to be home by dusk. After all, I was completely free all the daylight hours to go anywhere and do anything. Trusted to trust myself.

I looked around and saw that the nearest house was several fields away, so I set off to find someone there to take me home.

I sang and skipped across the fields, hearing no noise except my body moving through the grass. I climbed over two low ditches, and then over a metal gate, landing noisily on gravelly ground. The sound of that always startled but delighted me.

I walked over to the big timber door. The red paint was peeling, making it look beautiful in the evening light. It was an enormous house. I could just reach the door handle, so I stretched up and pulled it down and opened the door to a kitchen where Kitty Loftus was leaning over a line of lamps, lighting them for nightfall.

Kitty stepped back and threw out her arms, saying, 'Brenda, Brenda, Brenda. You're here again. It must be summertime.' She spread her arms as wide as they would go, saying, 'Come over here to me, my darling girl, come here, come here.'

I did. The hug she gave me nearly broke my back. She asked me what I had done with my day and told me not to worry, that Eamonn was above in the room and he'd come down to take me home to Nonee, safe and sound. With that she screamed Eamonn's name out so loud it blew my ear off.

Loud, clumsy noises from upstairs. Then the bold Eamonn appeared. I didn't know him all that well. I had seen him in the crowd of men that gathered at the back of the church on Sundays. For some reason, they became a gang, all scrubbed up with shaved and shiny faces, but they never actually went inside to Mass. I had marked him down as shy. So many Kerry men were shy.

He passed a window halfway down the stairs. His head was silhouetted against the light for just a flash, but long enough for me to hold my breath and drink in the beauty of the shape. His face. His smile.

'Brenda, Brenda, Brenda, now what are you doing out at this time of the night, eh? It's almost dusk. You know the rules. Your auntie will be worried. What delayed you?'

From someone else this would have been a reprimand, but there was so much laughter in his voice that I answered easily: 'I fell asleep in the long grass behind the well.'

'Ah yes,' he laughed. 'I know that spot. Indeed, I've fallen asleep there once or twice myself when I was gathering in the hay.'

'So now,' he said, 'there's four forms of transport for me to take you home safely to your lovely Auntie Nonee. There's the bicycle, the car, the donkey and the horse and cart. It's too long to take you sitting on the bar of the oul' bike. Poor Ted the donkey has been working all day long and he's tired out; Ted is in Killarney with the car. The cart is having the metal on both wheels replaced, which leaves us with Betty, my beautiful horse.'

I jumped up and down on the spot, saying, 'Oh yes, yes, yes, Eamonn, you know how much I love Betty!'

And I did love her. A huge, honey-coloured horse, unusual around there. She never seemed to do much work. The other horses did; I had seen them bringing milk to the creamery in Rathmore, working in the fields, making hay, ploughing. They were all dark-haired, unlike Betty, who seemed to have an easy time of it. She really was beautiful.

He tightened his trouser belt, then lifted me into the air as if I weighed as little as a feather. My tummy jumped and my pulse began to race. He swung me around his head, landing me perfectly onto his shoulders. I can't explain to you the mix of pleasures – visceral, visual and vocal – that took my body to another place whenever men did this with me.

Betty was shaking her head at us, nudging it out the half door of her shed. She was keen – I could see that – but not half as keen as I was. I had ridden on horseback before and I loved it.

Eamonn opened the bottom half of the door, coaxing Betty out across the yard to me. She was so big! I wasn't even as high as her belly. But she was happy and I felt it; I was happy and she felt it.

In another sweeping move, Eamonn lifted me up to the sky and plonked me down onto her back so firmly that I thought my body would split in two. I felt Eamonn jump on behind me. Betty was as quiet as a lamb, welcoming us aboard in her own inimitable way. Eamonn pulled me tight against his body, his right arm around my waist, his left reaching for the reins. I felt his thighs squeeze Betty's body as he spoke to her in loving tones. And off we went across the fields to home. I could feel Betty's backbone moving underneath me. Her pelt was warm and soft. My feet barely reached around her middle, but Eamonn held me tight and I felt free.

'I'm going the long way around,' he said, laughing into the dusk.

The sky was purple with evening light. The mountains moving far away. Eamonn's arms were huge, sunburned from working outside, and stinking of dirt. It was a heady smell. A smell I loved. A smell I'd chase all over Kerry. He tightened his arms, trapping me like a vice, then put my hands on Betty's mane and whispered with his mouth against my ear, 'Hold tight. Don't let go till I say the word.'

Betty's body rocked from side to side as we walked across the yard through a gap in the ditch and moved gently into a trot. I felt safe with Eamonn's arms around me. He balanced the movement as the ride shifted from a lazy trot to a gentle canter. Betty whinnied as we turned the corner, moving into a smooth gallop. I knew my hair was blowing into Eamonn's face. I didn't mind and nor did he. My happiness and trust in him were so complete that all I felt was love.

Now I knew the pleasure of no saddle. I could feel it; I could smell it as we galloped on through the open fields to home. There never was and never has been since a sense of safety, danger and love as there was on that enchanted ride.

Church

It was a balmy, lazy day. Therese had had to leave early to cycle into Rathmore for some sewing and knitting needles. Nonee would knit brightly coloured wool socks for us to wear with our wellingtons. They were cosy and warm and kept the cold of the rubber away from our feet. The only problem was that she couldn't knit the bit where the heel turned, which was very complicated. She'd knit as far as the heel and then leave them in the warm cupboard above the fireplace with all the knickers and the vests, which were kept gathered so that they'd be warm against our young skin on cold mornings. The socks would sit there until Bina arrived to bring us back to Dublin, because she could turn a heel, no bother. In fact, it was one of the few things that made her happy. She and Nonee would natter away while they were doing it. It was lovely to see the two of them together.

Gránia and I had been up in Casey's field all morning, just fooling around. Gránia was less bossy when it was just the two of us. I loved being alone with her. She was always interesting, questioned everything, and did not always accept the answers she was given. In fact, she usually didn't. Lazy baby me, I picked up most of my information second hand from her.

Gránia would stay that way all through her life. In fact, it would lead to one of the biggest mistakes my parents ever made when, after doing her Leaving Cert at the age of sixteen and receiving eight honours, Bina refused to let her go to Trinity College Dublin even though she had won a scholarship, because Trinity was a Protestant university and University College Dublin, where Bina wanted her to go, was Catholic. Gránia must have known this would happen. There'd be no celebration that she came first in all Ireland in the exams but, instead, a war began about going to the heretic college. My father, Des, always claimed to be an atheist, but he hid behind my mother. This one thing would haunt Gránia right up to the evening she went to bed early at the young age of sixty-eight and never woke up. A good death, for all that. I'm glad she died young.

But that day, we went over and sat on the ditch, which was covered with bright white daisies and yellow buttercups. We laughed together, both knowing these flowers were beautiful beyond words. We were completely free to do whatever we wanted to do, and go wherever we wanted to go, with one simple rule: be home by dusk. Sometimes we forgot, thinking that the restrictions of city life still cloaked our freedom.

I was in a floaty place, watching clouds again, when Gránia quietly asked, 'Is the church empty during the day?'

Although she spoke in her normal voice, now it seemed to boom out into the clean air.

'I think so,' I answered, imitating her voice. 'Old people,' I said, 'with little to do and no one to talk to. They wander in there. I know Father O'Brien does house visits to the sick during the day, so unless there are some old people, there shouldn't be anybody there. Why do you ask?'

She didn't answer. Nothing new there. Then, a few minutes later, she jumped up.

'C'mon, c'mon, follow me,' she said, and started walking purposefully towards the yard.

I hesitated, because I had just started making a daisy chain.

'Come *on*!' she cried, a mixture of impatience and command in her voice.

I dropped the flowers, jumped off the ditch and eagerly followed her. As I skipped and hopped along the road, I wondered what plan she had for us.

On that calm day, with its blue sky and fluffy clouds, I drank it all in, fully aware of how it made me feel. It was actually a great day to get water from the well. We could wash some of the endless stream of dirty clothes out the back of the house. A great drying day if we just scattered them over the bushes ...

Before the guilt kicked in, she had jumped over the wall into the yard.

'Stop dawdling!' she shouted. 'At least try to keep up!'

She moved fast and with intent from A to B. B was the school wall, where we sat on our hands, doing nothing at all. I saw a few wild poppies further along the road and made a mental note to pick them on the way home and put them in a mug of water for Nonee. We were opposite Annie Loftus's thatched cottage. She usually kept an open door for cakes and beautifully buttered bread, but not today.

'I have a plan, a dangerous one,' Gránia said mockingly. 'Are you in?'

She was laughing openly at me now.

'What is it?' I asked indignantly.

'*Aha*!' she said, giving me the devil's nose.

'Don't do that!' I said angrily. 'Stop bullying me. Then I'll see if I want to join in.'

'Forget it,' she answered.

So I did. I sat there, swinging my legs and whistling 'Que Será, Será'. It was the number-one song on the hospital requests programme on the radio. Doris Day had the voice of an angel, and I had what was called a 'crush' on her. I loved her voice and was consciously happy when I heard it.

Without warning, Gránia jumped off the wall.

'C'mon, c'mon,' she said. 'Follow me!'

I traipsed along behind her, way up the village past Kinnehan's farm. They had four sons in there. One of them, a red-haired lad, had a 'crush' on Gránia, which I found thrilling and she found boring.

We got to the end of the village, turned left and there it was: the village church, looming large against the small farmhouses. I always became a little nervous at the sight of it, but not Gránia. She walked over and pushed open the squeaking waist-high metal gate. I followed and she walked up to the entrance, pulled the very, very heavy door open, and in we went.

There is no silence like that of an empty church. It demands that you speak in whispers. Gránia waved me over to the back bench – or was it a pew? Was pew a Protestant word? She was super silent, which always thrilled me, as I knew this meant that great exploits were being planned.

She leaned over.

'Right,' she whispered, with her mouth touching my ear, 'now you take the left side, and I'll take the right. Look in every corner, every nook and cranny. We'll check to see if the place is totally, completely empty.'

I did as she commanded and didn't find a single soul any-where. I reported back in those very words and suddenly burst out laughing for no reason at all. Nerves. Ignoring me, she got up and stood in the central aisle, waving her hand to me to follow her as she walked very slowly up towards the altar.

There was a special pew allotted to each family. The McAuliffe pew was about halfway between the door and the altar, so not only was I aware that I had already broken one small rule, the butterflies in my stomach warned me that I could soon be committing one or two more sins.

Gránia lifted up a small cardboard box and gently raised the red velvet lid, revealing rows and rows of unblessed communion wafers. We froze. We stared, transfixed by how tightly and neatly packed they were. Together, we leaned over to smell them. Bread.

Suddenly, and to my complete horror, her hand appeared and fiddled around in the air. She leaned over, loosening one single wafer, which she then brought close up to her face. I was shaking like a leaf, waiting for thunder and fire to kill us for even touching the body of Christ. I was terrified of the blood I knew was going to squirt out from the box, from the crucifix, and from all of the pictures around us. The statues around the church should also all be bleeding by now, but nothing happened.

She moved the host towards my face for me to see it better. Curiosity beat the fear. I just wanted a peek. It was so ordinary looking and about the size of a shilling.

Brenda's First Holy Communion with Bina and Des.

Then she moved her hand and held the host inches from my face.

'Eat it,' she whispered, moving it closer to my lips.

'What?' I squeaked, trembling from head to toe.

'*Eat it*,' she repeated.

Dragging my thick, dry tongue around my mouth, I managed to squeal, 'Don't, Gránia. Please don't. For God's sake, stop this. I'll go straight to hell or we'll both be struck down dead! Oh God, Gránia … this is a *huge* sin. Think of the shame this'll bring on all of us, Mammy and Daddy as well. *Please* stop.'

But I could read her face. I knew exactly what she was going to do, and sure enough …

'You're such a wimp,' she mocked gleefully.

The smell of sin was all around us, mixed with the smell of religion. It made me sick.

'Watch,' she said.

Then, in slow motion, I saw her head fly back, her tongue slide out of her mouth and lie flat on her bottom lip. I saw her right hand arc high into the air, and then lower itself towards her tongue where, without hesitation, she placed the unblessed host. Then she spread her arms out in the shape of a crucifix and stood there, waiting for damnation. Impressed, I scrambled up and stood beside her, spreading my arms out exactly as she had done.

Nothing happened. Not even Satan seemed annoyed. Disappointed, Gránia took me by the shoulder and turned me around to face her. Her mouth was still open. I could still see the pieces of communion wafer, the body of God, melting on her stuck-out tongue. She started to laugh as she closed her mouth and said, 'I'm going to swallow it!'

She did.

I pushed my fists into my mouth to stop the screams escaping. I fell to the floor, flailing and wailing against the flames of hell that were about to engulf us. I kissed her feet, begging for forgiveness – for me, for her, for everything. I was rolling around on the floor in terror and disbelief. Then, in between my screams and tears, I saw that she was laughing and pointing at me.

'You're a terrible eejit,' she said. 'You should never listen to what grown-ups tell you. You believe everything they say. I believe nothing, and so far I've been right. I told you there was something fishy with this communion lark. It's just rice paper. It's just like those little cake things that Ruth's mother is always making from it. Remember? She makes yummy strawberry jam ones.'

I did remember.

'These are yummy too,' she said, as she stuffed handfuls of the wafers into the pockets of her shorts.

She might as well have kicked me in the face, I was so shocked. I stood transfixed, waiting for something dreadful to happen. But nothing whatsoever did. Nothing at all.

We sat down on the cold, tiled floor in a sullen, disappointed mood, both wondering the exact same thing: what was all this religion stuff about?

Then she got up and moved out of the sacristy into the altar area.

'C'mon, Brenda,' she beckoned, as she vaulted over the communion rails like a champion border collie. 'Come on, come on.'

Her voice sounded louder again under the high, arched ceiling of the nave. For a moment, we both stood still, struck by the echo. We'd have to calm down or we'd be heard all over the village. But, spurred on by her courage, and feeling that otherwise I was letting her down, I took a run at the communion rail and, to my surprise, I cleared it.

Now we were crossing in front of the tabernacle. We were aware of it, but we were ignoring it. Who or what was living in there now to come out and kill us? Nothing! I was growing less fearful. Of Gránia or of God or both? Secretly, I admired Gránia's disrespect for God.

'Let's light all the candles? What'cha think?' I said with a fake bravado, wanting to impress her.

'Fantastic!'

We ran over to the big round brass candle-holder. There was a large box of new candles underneath. You'd light a candle with an already-flaming one, and then slot it into a hole in the display area. This one was about half full, so we grabbed hand-fuls to fill it and then happily started lighting them. Playing with fire was always fun. We filled up every holder, stood back and looked at them, realizing that we hadn't put any pennies into the slot in the metal box. People put pennies in to buy a prayer. It seemed that if you paid for a prayer it would reach God's ears much faster.

Still, I was taken aback. The array of candles did look beauti-ful. I had never seen it so full, and it was like a golden cloud of flame, illuminating the pious pictures, the stained-glass windows, the silver and gold on the altar, and the diamonds shining in the tabernacle door. The whole spectacle over-whelmed me. I was overcome. Gránia noticed, as she always did. She put her arm around me to calm me down.

Rebels at rest, we flopped back into a pew. Gránia lay down. She was sucking her thumb. Bina hit her when she did that, but I knew that it comforted her. God knows, it was hard to rein in her extraordinary energy. Gránia felt threatened all her life, but I knew that sucking her thumb meant she was happy and she was planning.

I felt supremely happy but then out of the blue I wanted to have a wee. My overactive bladder interrupting as usual.

'Hang on!' I said. 'Hang on. I'll go out the back door through the sacristy. I'll be back in a min.'

But before I even stood up I changed my mind.

'Watch me,' I said boldly, walking out of the pew and towards the altar. 'Watch me! I have a great idea! The best idea ever!'

Gránia went quiet. Delighted with this, and drunk with my idea, I went back to the big candle holder, turned around near the burning candles, and said, 'Follow me.' And to my surprise, she did.

Below the candle holder there was a big round container to catch the wax dripping from the burning candles. As I stood and smiled at Gránia, I spread my legs, reached behind, flung out the skirt of my dress, caught the corners into my body, and pulled my knickers down. I leaned back a bit and peed loudly over the melted wax.

'Oh my God, Brenda!' said Gránia. 'That's mad! That's mad!'

She then followed suit, grinning from ear to ear and emptying her bladder, surprising us both with a big fat fart, which slipped out of her bum and echoed like a trumpet around the church.

After we had emptied ourselves, we waited. Had we gone too far now? If I was not struck down after this, then Gránia had been right all along. But again, nothing happened. By now we were both exhausted.

Seeking another fix, my eye fell on the pulpit. That was where all the drama happened, where a man dressed up as a priest told you every Sunday that you were a lost soul. I climbed the high steps into it, but was far too small to see over the edge.

'I can't see you!' Gránia shouted.

I looked around, saw a tasselled cassock, pulled it towards me, and stood on it. Now my head was just above the rim of the pulpit.

'Can you see me clearly?' I asked.

'Yes, yes,' said Gránia.

But I couldn't see all of her. With the strength of Tarzan, I grabbed the leather-clad rim of the pulpit and pulled myself up until I was sitting on it with my legs dangling.

'Give me a sermon!' she said, in that voice I was afraid to ignore.

'Okay,' I said. 'Jesus was born in the year one. The Virgin Mary was his mother and St Joseph was his father and they had a donkey ... AND the devil was born in the year two. He hates Jesus and all Catholics.'

I was so tired by now. I lay my head upon my elbow, saying to myself: 'O, to have a little house, to own the hearth and stool and all, the heaped up sods upon the fire, the pile of turf against the wall. To have a clock with weights and chains, and pendulum swinging up and down, a dresser filled with shining delph, speckled and white and blue and brown ...'

Poetry always calmed me, and even though I was talking quietly, I could hear Padraic Colum's poem echoing all around the church. I caught Gránia's eye as she listened intently. We both loved poetry and we were enjoying this.

Thrilled to hear Gránia joining in, I listened to our voices speak as one the simple truth and sadness of the poem. Gránia was lying on a pew now, flat on her back, arms behind her head, gazing at the magnificent ceiling as if for the first time as she picked up the lines. She had a lovely speaking voice. I tingled all over at the sound of both of our voices inside the church. The rhythm of the words soothed our over-excited bodies. The echoes gave way to silence. We had spoken truth together. Something I felt was not often spoken in this beautiful church.

I realized that Gránia was uneasy. She went deathly quiet and I jumped down from the pulpit and joined her. I sat beside her. She stood up, took both my hands in both of hers, and kissed me formally on my forehead.

'*That* was prayer, Brenda,' she said. 'That was *real* praying. Not the rubbish we hear here on Sundays.'

That moment is too beautiful to forget. As I write, I remember how she took my hand and walked me down the aisle and back out into the warm sunny day, both of us knowing that something significant had happened between us.

Still hand in hand, we walked around to the back of the church. The warmth and strength I felt from her hand around mine was special in its rarity. I think that me loving her so much frightened her. Years later, she would tell me how desperate I was, as a child, to offer my love to anyone, how my need to be loved back was written large across my face, making her realize she could never give me what I needed.

We hugged and smiled easily now. We danced for a while, feeling joy, delight and freedom from everything that we were leaving behind. The church no longer scared me; it had never scared her.

Bedwetting

I don't remember my parents ever sleeping in the same room, never mind the same bed. Gránia and I were in the front bedroom, a big double bed for us. My mother in the back room, a big double bed for her. My father in the box room, a small single bed for him.

There were times when, for no apparent reason, my mother would bring me into her bed to sleep with her. When things were good, I loved it. I would snuggle up against her bony back, relishing the heat from her slim body. I would wrap my little arms around her, delirious with happiness at the gentle physical contact. But even in that happiness, there was a worry. Instinctively, I knew that my father should be lying where I was. He should be holding her body against his, kissing her neck, enticing her to sleep. This was *his* place, not mine. The thought never lingered long enough to interrupt my pleasure, but it niggled.

I was a champion bedwetter, the cause of which, in those days, wasn't really understood. To give my parents credit, they eventually took me to the Meath Hospital to have it checked out. No cure, they were told.

Today, I almost shake as I write and remember the dread I felt when I woke up in the night and felt the cold wet bed beneath me. I would lie there, trembling from head to toe, dreading my mother waking up to the wetness. Sometimes the wet went as far over as the edge of her nightdress. It must have been unpleasant for her but, as usual, the punishment didn't fit the crime. Sometimes I would get away with her awful verbal abuse, or a slap on the face, and being ignored for the rest of that day. But sometimes she would wake to feel the damp and, in a flash, go completely mad. She would drag me out of the bed and scream at me to rip all the sheets off while she went to collect the big laundry basket. She threw it into the bed at me, hissing into my face that I should put the filthy sheets into it, bring them to the bathroom and fill the bath with hot water.

Scared to death and shaking like a leaf, I fumbled around with the sheets. They were the size of tents in a small child's hands. I can still hear the low, weak moaning, like that of a frightened dog, that came from my throat as I knew now that I was doomed to be given one of the most hideous punishments in my mother's repertoire.

The bath rim was level with my chest. I had to stand on tiptoe to see into the bath properly. I couldn't get in or out alone yet. I could barely reach the taps. On those occasions, I would pull myself up onto the lip and walk, tightrope style, the three steps necessary to fall against the hand basin, where I would lean and get my balance right. If I could sit on the side of the hand basin, with my feet on the bath lip, by leaning across I could just about reach the far tap and turn it on. The nearby tap was easy. I enjoyed the climbing, despite my terror.

When both taps were on, feebly dribbling out hot and cold water, I would climb back down and drag the soiled sheets, inch by inch, over the pretty flowers on the landing carpet floor and across onto the black-and-white tiled bathroom floor. Then I would heave them, bit by bit, up and over and into the bath. It was exhausting. All the while, my mother would stand over me, telling me loudly, over and over again, to hurry up. How disgusting I was, she said, how sinful. I would burn in hell for wetting the bed.

Many years later, helping to drag fishing nets from the ocean back into a trawler, the exact replica of those movements caused a cold shudder down my back on the warmest summer day.

I don't remember anyone ever coming to help me. My father and my sister were in rooms inches from where this was going on. Many years later, when Gránia and I were grown up, I asked them why. They both said they never heard a thing. I don't believe them. Perhaps Gránia didn't. My ever-present active protector was, indeed, an unusually heavy sleeper who snored a lot. Maybe she didn't hear. But my father? Why did he say that he never heard, never knew that his wife was beating the shit out of one of his daughters? How come he never sensed the sickly smell of violence in the air inside the room, in the small house where all this was happening? Didn't see through the outrageous and ridiculous reasons my mother spluttered out if he spotted a scratch or a bruise on me that made no sense? He just didn't understand? I don't believe he didn't hear the bedwetting punishments in the middle of the night. I still can't believe him.

The treatment I received for wetting the bed was one of the three or four serious forms of violence I experienced as a child. I'm convinced that that violence led to the later violence of my first suicide attempt. I carry it with me to this day. There are still times when, because of the buried guilt and shame, I find it difficult to leave the house.

Dreams

Iwoke up from my dream and ran to where Des was sleeping in the back room. My shoulders were about the same height as the bed and I was able to slide my arms in under the covers to touch him.

'Don't die! Don't die!' I screamed.

He was lovely to me that time. He pulled his bedclothes back and sat me on the bed beside him.

'I am going to die eventually,' he said, 'but not tonight.'

He brought me to my own bed and tucked me in.

'Sleep now,' he said. 'Sleep now. I'll still be here tomorrow.'

Unbearable

If I touched the little collar on the neck of her nightdress, Bina wouldn't wake. A pale pink rose. I touched it and stuck my fingers in my mouth to stop myself from screaming.

I lay back and put my legs up in the air to relax.

I rolled back like a ballet dancer and touched the rose there on her pink neck. Pink looked good on Bina.

But then my body froze as I got closer and saw the wee, small stitches of repair all around her beautiful pink rose. Tears fell down my cheeks. Had she done this?

She didn't sew. She did knit, she did bake, but she didn't sew.

Did she love this rose as much as I did? Did she repair her pretty nightdress on her own because she knew how much it meant to me? Did she love me *this much*?

The unbearable intimacy of the situation made me reach down and hold her small hand. I stroked it in terror, half-hoping that she'd wake up and kill me.

Brenda's first day at school.

Blood on the Stones
(Meath Hospital)

Bina and Des were whispering, which was never good news for me. I had overheard them the night before, saying I had to go to the Meath Hospital again. I was about five years old, and every Tuesday my mother and I would get up at around six in the morning. Why was never explained to me, other than that I had go into the Meath Hospital for the whole morning, and Bina would come and collect me at lunchtime. Nothing more. It was exciting getting up in the dark – there was no light at all – going down the park and waiting at the bus stop, but I was nervous. Was I going to die? Is that why I was being taken to hospital?

Des never did these trips. It was always Bina. Looking back, it was simple selfishness on his part, a way of escaping responsibility. I was always uncomfortable with it. It was one of the many things that made me feel what a bloody nuisance my body was to both of them. As though my body was separate from me. My body was what caused all the trouble. I didn't know how to separate myself from my body.

This particular day it was pitch black, almost as dark as Gneeveguilla, and with no help from the street lamps early in the morning. Although I was fed up and worrying, as usual, there was that stillness in the air that tightened my gut with excitement. But much as I loved the dark, I didn't want to go to that hospital again.

Why didn't he drive me? He drove me everywhere. Bina and I had to make three or four different bus journeys to get there while he just swanned around in his lovely car. He hadn't even taught her how to drive. I felt crossness mixing with my tiredness as he sat in the kitchen, wrapped up in the dressing gown he loved so well. 'Warm winter wool,' he'd say, smiling and patting the pocket, which held a pack of Carroll's cigarettes and a Zippo. 'Foxford wool.' He was sitting at the small kitchen table having a cup of tea with, as always, a copy of the *Irish Times* leaning against the milk jug, folded over to the crossword puzzle. His morning ritual.

'*Never* interrupt your father when he's doing the crossword.' So I didn't. '*Never* interrupt your father when he's typing.' So I didn't. And '*Never ever* interrupt your father when he's "thinking".' 'Thinking' was when he'd hang his head back and close his eyes, as if asleep.

Des was a journalist for the *Irish Times*. It was a Very Important Job. He also had a radio show, under the name Fred Desmond, called *Down the Country*. He was a city boy but he'd grown to love the countryside on his frequent trips out of Dublin to go fishing. Most country people didn't have electricity yet, and listened to big radios that had huge batteries that needed to be brought to town periodically to be charged.

'He's *thinking*,' my mother would hiss at me. 'He's sick and tired of your carry-on. You have the man exhausted. For God's sake, let him have his bit of thinking.'

Dad looked up from the crossword, saying, 'I can't pick you up at lunchtime.'

'That's fine,' my mother answered quickly.

'Do you need a torch?' he asked.

'Ah no, sure we'll be grand,' she said. But she was nervous. I could tell.

With that, she put one of my 'good' coats on me and we stepped out into the black morning. I immediately relaxed. I felt the darkness wrap itself around me, sheltering me from God knows what – the fearful and unknown, perhaps? As always, my mother walked quickly, pulling me along behind. I dilly-dallied on purpose, just to annoy her.

We crossed the main road, sat on Mrs Hackett's garden wall, and waited for a 48, 48A, or 44 bus to come. It was quiet. Silent. I noticed how huge the sky is without stars. I whistled quietly just to throw the sound out into the dark silence. It was lovely; the sound made the silence quieter.

Immediately, I felt a whack across the back of my head.

'Stop that whistling! I've told you a hundred times, Our Lady cries when girls whistle. *And* it's a sin, so don't forget to tell the priest on Saturday.'

The quiet was ruined, so I took the easy way out and sulked. I knew this irritated her.

The bus came, a no. 48, and Jolly Jim was on this morning. He was great; he used to let me swing out of the pole when the bus was moving. This was totally forbidden, as it was very dangerous. That's exactly why I liked it. It felt like flying.

We sat like soldiers as far as Kelly's Corner, where we got off and walked quickly through the light of street lamps and around a corner into Camden Street. Halfway down, we turned sharp left into a tiny narrow lane, a short cut up to the main gate of the Meath. I had always been driven by my father on trips into town so this was new to me.

The footpath was so thin we couldn't walk abreast. She went ahead and I went behind. There was a high green wooden door on my left, flakes of dead paint hanging on to let you know that it once had been bright green. I fell in love with it.

Under a small gap, there was a little ribbon of cobblestones flowing out. Feigning tiredness, I sat on the pavement, bending over to see under the enormous door. The cobblestones felt great: smooth, round, warm and wet. As I slid my hand across one of them, I felt a shock of instant intimacy. Then I heard the smallest distant sound. It stopped me in my tracks. I dropped a little stone I had picked up. I knew that sound: fear. Fear of someone, of something. Suddenly, I coughed up sick into my hands before they moved to my ears to stop the sudden sound of terror. I fell onto the kerb, bent over.

'What's going on in there?' I cried. 'That's pain. Who's in pain?

'It's animals!' I screamed then. 'They're killing animals!'

'Of course they are, for God's sake, it's an abattoir,' my mother said impatiently.

'Why, why? Why are they in pain? Why are they killing them?' I cried.

'For us to eat, of course!' she barked.

I put my hands around my head, pulled it down between my knees, and cried for all the pain around me. I opened my eyes and saw silk-like threads of red liquid snaking their way around the cobbles, close enough for me to rest my face against them, for me to smell the dark, pungent smell: a smell I would grow to love, a smell that would never, ever leave my life after that first time on those cobblestones.

Leaning closer still, I watched my tears falling on the cobblestones, mixing with the blood that glistened in the morning sun, turning everything red. Blood. Red blood. Animal blood. The blood of pain. I pressed my little hands hard down onto the cobblestones, allowing this potent mix to flow between my fingers: the feel, the smell, how lovingly the blood embraced each cobble. I placed one hand flat onto the blood and felt a shiver down my spine as the sickly-sweet smell engulfed me. The smell was all there was. I breathed the smell deeply. I could taste it now. A reassuring metal mixed with a sort of sweetness. I was mesmerized. I felt the still-warm blood move across my fingers. It was the sweetest thing I had ever known. I moved my fingers back and forth until my hand was drenched in blood. I felt its warmth, and it gave me instant peace.

From far away, I could hear my mother calling: 'Brenda, Brenda, for goodness' sake c'mon, or we'll be late!'

Still I sat there, mesmerized, watching the thick bright-red blood caressing every cobble as it flowed. I sucked in the smell and, instantly, I understood everything: animals, pain, fear, blood, death.

My mother called again to hurry me up but I sat frozen on the spot, feeling faint and weak, dizzy with the visceral effect. My mother's voice was distant as I slid my hand down to touch the cobbles again. She walked back to drag me on.

'Get up, get up!' she said.

I pushed my hands down on the cobbles to lift my body up and slipped, sprawling across the bloodied cobbles as my mother screamed.

'Your coat!' she shouted. 'Jesus Christ, Brenda, your good new coat! Get up on your feet, for God's sake. Get up, get up!'

I heard her as I laid my cheek against the blood and felt at peace. Roughly, she pulled me up, gasping at the sight of my bloody face. She spat on her fingers and started to clean me up. She did this a lot and I found it utterly disgusting: rub, rub, rub, spit, spit, spit; the stink of it. I had to clench my fists to stop myself from hitting her in the face. She rummaged in her handbag, pulling out one of my father's hankies, spat on that, and wiped away the dead cow's blood.

Without her seeing, I skimmed a little blood into my palm and held it there until it dried. Then I stood up and walked on to the dreaded hospital. I hid the blood for half that day. My first relationship with blood had brought me a new power. A new friend. Little did I know that that first touch of blood on the cobblestones would lead to a beautiful, dangerous love affair.

*

The hospital smelled clean. There was disinfectant everywhere, an insult to the nose. A doctor arrived with two swan-head nurses and said hello/goodbye to Bina, who ran off into the dark morning to make her way by bus across to Mount Argus to catch the early Mass, and then on to Milltown to teach her first class at 9 a.m. When she had left, they brought me down some stairs and through a very long, very quiet corridor. We went through a high door that led into a long, thin rectangular room. It was a ward for sick people, with a different smell. I didn't recognize it and I didn't like it. There must have been twenty beds with very old people in them. I felt sorry for them. It made me wish again that I had a granny or a grandad like other girls, but mine had died young, I was told.

I was left standing there as the doctors and nurses talked together in a bunch, ignoring me. As I looked around, I realized that these were not just very old, sick people; they were very old, sick, *dying* people. Dear God, was *I* dying? Were they going to kill me? I felt utter panic and fear. The doctor turned around and marched me down to the end of the ward where a screen had been set up around a bed, cutting off the other beds. I was told to take my clothes off.

'What?!'

'Come, come now, the doctor doesn't have all day!'

Mortified, I pulled my dress over my head, then my vest. I was so ashamed. Nobody other than Bina and Gránia had seen me naked – in the bath, on Saturday nights. I closed my eyes and peeled my knickers down over my legs, stumbling as I dragged them over my shoes, utterly embarrassed. I stood there shaking, terrified of what they might do to me.

'On the bed now, young lady. Hurry up!'

I lay down on the bed, ready to die and go to hell, and then they terrified me by pushing my legs apart, hurting me. Next a large man stretched out his large right hand and, leaning over me, he stuck two of his fingers hard and rough right up into me, into where my pee came out. I screamed at him but he just pushed my knees further apart. I screamed again. His voice was high and shrill as he told me to be still and, out of sheer terror, I obeyed. I knew that he was going to pull my insides out. Why? What had I done wrong? I had stolen biscuits. He was squeezing my insides and murmuring to himself and I knew that he was going to kill me. Was that because I had climbed the forbidden tree the other day?

'Oh Jesus, Jesus, Baby Jesus, I'm sorry, please save me now!'

He reached across to what I would later learn was a kidney tray. The nurse was holding a long syringe filled with brown-coloured water, which she handed to Dr Lane, as I discovered this big intimidating man was called. He pushed it right up where his fingers had been. The sting, the pain, made me scream again and slam my knees together, causing everything to fall out and clatter onto the floor, the needle scratching my inner thigh on the way.

'Stop it!' the nurse told me loudly. 'Stop that. You're a very bold girl. You've upset Dr Lane now, you stupid little girl.'

'Mammy! Daddy! Gránia!' I cried out louder, in mortal fear for my life. 'Help, help me please, they're killing me!'

'*Stop!*' she shouted at me. 'You've disturbed half the patients now. You're a bold, bold, bold girl. Just lie still and let the doctor do his work. You're a very lucky girl indeed to have Dr Lane. He's the best in the country, so stay quiet now.'

I tried to stay quiet, gasping for air. I let him spread my legs and come at me again with a new syringe refilled, needle replaced.

'Look at the state of you now,' the nurse sneered.

Dr Lane mumbled something to himself and then stuck the needle in again. Then, very quickly, they pushed a thin red rubber tube right up where his fingers had been. They attached it to a plastic bag, which hung from the side of the bed. He smiled.

'There now!' he said. 'Wasn't that grand!'

He wasn't asking me. It was a statement.

As they walked away, I lay there crying my eyes out and begging for someone – Mammy, Daddy, Gránia. Where were they? Didn't they know what the doctor was doing to me? He was killing me!

Exhausted now, I fell into a troubled sleep only to be woken by soft coughing. The nurse was right, yes, I had woken the old people up from their half-dead sleep. I could hear coughing and spitting and moaning. The old man in the bed the other side of my screen said, 'try to sleep'. They'd left the screen to give me privacy.

I had had my funny bits forced open and felt fear beyond fear and now there was a small trickle of blood running down my leg. The cow's blood was still on my hand. I sniffed at it, I tried to rub it away, but the moment I saw my blood on my hands, mixed now with blood from the cobblestones, I knew at once that I was going to die here. I took some comfort, then, from the dead cow's blood mixed with mine. Now the cows were mine, my friends. Their blood was mine, and mine was theirs.

The ward went quiet once more, no more spitting and moaning. Hours of silence went by before an old man's weak voice asked, 'What's your name?'

'Brenda.'

'Well, welcome, Brenda, to St Mary's Ward. Why are you here? What's wrong with you?'

'I don't know.'

'Don't be a smarty pants … you can't be worse than us. Why are ya here?'

'Don't know!' I shouted, breaking into floods of tears, which caused bells to ring and everyone to shout until another big face came around the corner of the screen, grunting at me that I must never shout like that again, to stop looking for attention while upsetting all the old people in the room, who wouldn't sleep at all now because of me. She smiled an evil smile, pulled up the sheet, forced my legs apart and pulled the tube out. It felt like a stick of thorns. She threatened me, shouted at me to stop crying and be still, washed the rubber tube then shoved it up my tiny urethra again, as she smiled and I bled.

I kissed the blood on my hand, finding there such comfort that I was overcome. Obviously I was going to die, but why this way? Would I die alone? Without Daddy, Mammy, Gránia? Why had they just dumped me here this morning?

Nothing but the blood would soothe me. I rubbed my fingertips into the tiny trickle. I put my finger in my mouth. The taste was beautiful, the feel of it like red velvet. It was still warm. I pushed my hand into my vagina, swiped up some of the remaining drops, and rubbed them on my tongue. My own warm blood mixed with salt was a taste unsurpassed. It calmed me down.

Another nurse came hours later. She looked shocked and talked angrily to herself as she washed the bloody tube again and washed the blood away from my vagina and thighs. She was so gentle, pleading with me that if ever that nurse tried to do this procedure again to shout my head off.

Des Shouts

Des jumped up and shouted at me. I had never even heard him raise his voice before, but somehow I had known that, if ever it was going to happen, it would be now, at the morning ritual of brushing out the knots and tangles in my waist-length curly hair to braid it into two long plaits for school, to please the nuns. Bina certainly didn't hold back; she'd drag the strong steel hairbrush she'd bought in Clery's from the hairline on my forehead right over the top of my head and down through the long length of twists and knots, right down through the golden curls to my waist. When there wasn't one knot left from the day before she would stroke the golden sheet with her red, uncared-for hands and smile at it. My hair was her pride and joy and though those same sad hands regularly beat the shit out of me, I loved the peaceful look that came not just over her face, but over all of her when someone complimented her on her daughter's beautiful golden hair.

I had interrupted Des's concentration on whatever bloody book he was reading. I hated the way he'd put his finger on the word on the line he had reached if you tried to talk to him. 'What is it?' he'd ask. It made me feel as though I had broken an invisible glass wall that surrounded him. The only time I can remember being aware of him sharing his happiness was on the bank of some river he was fishing in. Fishing for trout and salmon was his source of ecstasy.

Des was a handsome man – intelligent, thoughtful at times, and so curious, always asking questions. He was always jumping into the car and driving towards Dundrum village to turn left at Carvill's chemist and screech to a halt outside the small library. He would run inside, be there for twenty minutes or so, and then come out, stumbling with the bundle of ten or twenty books he'd borrowed. Whenever possible, I went with him. Driving to the library was something I really wanted to do with him. I would wait outside in the car, but I wanted to carry the returning books and wait for the taking-out ones. I loved the library, which was a funny shape, sitting there alone in the middle of a green field.

Waking

I had fallen asleep in the old armchair in the kitchen and woke to find the paraffin lights being lit by Auntie Nonee. I fell into line behind Gerard to get a light to bring up to the bedroom. The smell of paraffin was intoxicating. I would push my nose into the rag when nobody was looking and breathe in. Instant giddiness. The queue moved slowly, as it was dangerous, but I would reach Nonee and she would light the wick with a little flame on the end of a small stick and pass me the shining glass globe that fitted neatly into a slit in the metal base. Then we'd all scatter to carefully place the lamps around the house. There were two beside the door – one for going outside if there was no wind and one for going upstairs to bed.

Nonee knew that I slipped outside sometimes, just to lean against the wall and drink in the pitch-black Kerry air that made each star a hundred times brighter than any star you'd see from my bedroom window in the city. Eventually, Nonee would come out, stand with me for a while, and then take my hand and bring me in. Dear God, how much love that gave me! My hand in hers. My life safe in her hand. The rough skin on her fingers, the softness of her palm. I could have walked around the world and back holding hands with her.

Once inside, she'd slip her hand away to pick up the big main lamp that would stay downstairs when she had us all tucked up. Eleven steep steps. Yelps of joy when we reached the top. There were four small bedrooms, one of which was used as a sort of dry storeroom, one for Nonee, and for Bina when she was down from Dublin, one for the two boys, and Des when he was down, and one for us ... the girls, the seven girls!

The bed was a big single or perhaps a small double with big posts and a sinking hairy mattress with old clothes – coats, old jackets, sacks, cardigans, anything to keep you warm and happy – piled at the end of it. All the days since then, I have never felt such joyous freedom, such utter abandon as in that girls' room. Of course, we started off with pillow fights, which would lead on to God knows what. Gránia was always a leader, so she coupled up with Therese, the eldest of the girls, who had a fondness for bullying. I hung out with Deirdre, who was the same age as me and by far the funniest of us all. We were opposing armies but, in truth, Deirdre and I were nervy about Gránia and Therese. Gránia was startlingly inventive with her so-called 'games', and so to war we'd go every night, singing songs and playing tin whistles for each other. On and on we'd go until, one by one, we'd fall asleep still dressed, pulling up the old coats, the worn woollen rugs, old dry sacks, old cardigans and sweaters, anything under which we could curl up until we fell asleep. We were a bundle of beautiful, happy, sleeping children, arms and legs loosely wrapped around one another with an abandon that only sleeping children can show. We lay loosely hugging until the morning. Seven bodies would unfurl in changing patterns. At least one of them – me – thumping with excitement, dragging on clothes and racing to the hen-house to push my fingers in under the red hen's belly, stroking the warmth of the feathers as I slid my hand in slowly to feel for an egg. Shouting loudly so they'd hear me in the kitchen, I informed them we had two beautiful brown eggs from the red hen, which just now had almost died of fright when I shouted, 'She's laid two! She's laid two absolute beauties!' I picked them up carefully and carried them, nestled in my hands, into the house and up into the brown egg bowl on the table.

Nonee's husband, my Uncle Ritchie, died when Therese was twelve. I remember those weeks so clearly, as I remember Kay Geddess, Gránia's friend who died of tuberculosis and whose dead body I had seen in her coffin. I had been fascinated by Kay's body. Now that I had heard of Uncle Ritchie's death my first thought was, *Great! We'll have to go to Gneeveguilla for an extra trip!*

My mind began to race. Uncle Ritchie had been the local carpenter and made all the coffins for the bodies around the area. Would he be buried in a coffin he'd made himself? Oh no, no! That was wrong. And then – what else? – Des couldn't get off work to drive us down, so we took the train from Dublin and changed at Mallow Junction to the train for Killarney, where Tim Sullivan would be waiting for us in his car.

By the time we got there, Ritchie had been waked and his body lay in a closed wooden coffin waiting to be put in the graveyard. Everybody came. Farmers in their old tweed suits, smelling of manure. They were all there. I can still see the crowd waiting outside Nonee's house. And Nonee's sad calm as we followed Uncle Ritchie's coffin, borne aloft on the shoulders of six farmers, the short distance to his grave. A distance about twice as long as the small city street I live on now.

Back, left to right: Jocelyn (a friend of Des), Nonee, Uncle Ritchie, Grandma Murphy. Front: Brenda, Gránia, Therese. Deirdre is little girl in front with Gránia's arms around her.

Killing the Pig

I loved pigs. I still love pigs.

There used to be one, sometimes two, in a pen beside the hay-barn up against the field wall. A low fence of broken tree branches ran around an area of ten square feet. There was a lot of hay on the ground. You could sit on the fence and chat to the pigs.

I used to jump over the fence and stroke them. The beautiful short white hair on their velvety smooth pink skin. I would kiss their piggy little ears and pull their piggy little tails and look into their piggy little eyes and talk to them.

Their grunts were music on the air, the clear and empty Kerry air. They had a wicked sense of humour and their grunts were easy on my ears.

I wasn't supposed to play with them. Certainly not to jump over the fence and hug them. But they had a great sense of fun. Nonee wasn't too keen on my playing with them but she would just smile her serious smile and wink at me.

I never saw pigs mating but I saw a sow giving birth. The atmosphere when she was ready to deliver was – as with almost everything on a small farm – tense with excitement and worry. A couple of men from above the village would arrive to help Nonee out. She had no husband but everybody helped her and somehow everything got done well.

When the sow started to deliver there was no screaming. She just lay on her side as one piglet after another slid smoothly out of her. They poured out quickly and easily. They were covered in slimy grey stuff, which you had to wipe off them. They arrived at what seemed the speed of light. When cleaned up, they would jump into the air. They would *dance*, making it difficult to carry them. You could actually see them grow little white hairs along their body, pushing their way into the world, making it impossible not to hug them, kiss them, and hug and kiss them again.

Quite quickly they made their way to their mother's breasts, nudging each other to get a drink. I'd stay there, loving them, until it was dark. I'd back out the door and down the two steps, fully aware of the holiness of it all. Babies in a manger sleeping on the straw. But I loved these babies so much more than that other one everyone talked about.

*

Then *that* day arrived.

We'd all help to scrub the kitchen table and then we'd carry it out to the yard, around the corner of the house, placing it firmly on the ground between the big hay-barn and the end wall. The men had lengths of rope, which they skilfully attached to each table leg. They tied big country knots, leaving the loose ends to fall gracefully to the ground, not knowing when they'd come in useful.

That's when the show began.

Each man expertly grabbed a pig leg.

That's when the screaming began.

They would drag the mother pig out down the two steps across the yard and swing her high in the air before slamming her down on the table on her back. I swear I heard her spine break as she screamed ten inches from my face, mesmerizing me. Then, with brutal speed, her four legs were dragged to each corner and with no regard for the tearing muscle and the breaking bones they would tie each leg to a corner of the table until it was well-anchored and ready for a swift slaughter more violent than anything you could imagine in your worst nightmare.

I hear it now. I smell it now.

They cut the throat first, deep enough to cut the head almost completely off. They jumped back fast to avoid the sudden spurting blood. They leaned across the shoulder. They held the knife high before slashing deep, deep down the full length of the body, ripping it apart from neck to anus, showing not the slightest pity for the screaming body now twitching weakly on the table.

Covered in warm blood, I bent to touch the head, hanging by a thread. It was a piteous thing.

All gentleness was gone now and what I saw were people working to satisfy the daily hunger of mankind.

My small and bloodied hand flew to my mouth to stop me shouting out. I put my arms around its head, looked into its dying eyes, and saw a peace that made me gasp.

I poured the pig's splashing blood into a bucket and immersed myself up to the elbows in the innards so that I could remove the bladder and blow it up like a balloon.

I held my hands, red with the blood, up to the sky.

Forge

L eaning idly against the door of the little forge, I watched
Michael Óg shoe the horse. I breathed in the hot, steamy
smells and again my body felt that throbbing awareness of
being alive.

I never understood those middle years of adulthood. People
were young or old, and Michael Óg was in the middle. He had
a pleasing face with snow-white hair that sat in uneven lumps
on his head. That should have been funny but it wasn't, it
was just interesting. Like all Kerry men, he had a ready smile
and warmth about him, which was now being tested with the
sweat spreading all over his face and down his big brown arms
with the shirtsleeves rolled up. He gripped the tongs so nimbly,
placed the horseshoe on the thin bench, and then started
beating it into the proper shape for this particular horse. He
held it over the flames until it was bright hot red and then he
swung the tongs high through the air and into a barrel full of
cold water, where the shoe made a loud hissing noise, as if a
thousand snakes were hiding in the walls. Ah! The perfection
made me jump and shout, 'Yes, yes!' as he lifted out the now-
grey shoe and, with another swoop, brought it back towards
the horse, and freeing one hand, grasped the horse's back leg
and brought the horseshoe down onto its foot.

I passionately wished I could do what Michael Óg did. I desperately wanted to do all the men's jobs on the farm, and most of the time they were generous and either let me help in some small way or invented a job for me. Last year, Michael had let me plunge the glowing red shoe into the barrel of cold water, causing an instant loud hiss as clouds of hot steam filled the forge. I could hardly hold the tongs, but he trusted me, so I squeezed them until the steam settled down and then held the horseshoe up in the air. He nodded quickly and ducked under the horse's huge body. He grabbed the back left leg with one hand, while pulling over a stool with the other. Then – as neatly as you can imagine – he sealed the steaming shoe perfectly onto the horse's hoof. The sound and smell of singeing almost made me faint.

Forge 2

Turn right out of Nonee's door and leaning up against the wall of her house was a big shed which was the blacksmith's. Séan Óg, as he was called, was about twenty and Michael's only son. His father had run the forge before him, had worked in extreme heat and the half dark for hours and hours each day for years. There was no electricity in the forge or the house.

There was always a line of donkeys and horses tied to a rail standing there, quite content that their owners had tied them up and then left them there while they pissed off up the village for a pint. Indeed, there were many times when I would burst out laughing at the sight of old Joe or Johnny from above beyond the bog coming back at the very end of an afternoon, singing and chatting with each other, all the better for their long pints in Callaghan's pub. I loved it when they were drunk. They'd roar with laughter at nothing and everything, their voices raised not to shouting level but not far below. I always knew that they were happy. They'd play with me, tickle me, give me pennies, halfpennies, money they didn't have, to spend on sweets in Timmy Taidy's across the road. They'd break into song, giving great respect to the slow, sad ones, and beaming toothless smiles at the happy airs. Sometimes there'd be a step of a dance, a little jig maybe. Just a dance down the road as they went to pick up their faithful re-shod animals.

Séan was usually getting ready to go up the road for his pint when they got back from theirs. There'd be a quiet, intense mumbling between the lot of them. In a neat huddle, hands would be dipping deep into trouser pockets, feeling the inside of jacket pockets, just going through the ritual really, because each one of those men was as sharp as a razor. Each one of those men knew how much they owed Séan today and yesterday, so whatever deal had been agreed, back God knows when, was just being acted out. And I understood all of it.

Séan was another good-looking Kerryman with jet-black curly hair, white teeth, and sallow skin. In my adult life, travelling the world from New York to Sydney, and meeting many handsome men, none of them had the charm of that slow, sleepy smile coupled with those clear blue eyes that Kerrymen and Connemara men have in spades. I remember them all as young gods.

The other great thing about Séan – well, two great things, really: he'd actually let me help him – like *properly* help him – in the forge; and he'd pull me up on my Kerry accent.

I used to lean against the ever-open filthy forge door, chatting and watching him re-shoe horses and donkeys. I knew he found my being at the door distracting, so he'd always call me over. That's how I got involved in helping him. By the age of ten, I was practically able to shoe a horse myself. Health and safety wouldn't even let me lean on the door today. When Séan had an old horse or a quiet donkey, he'd turn his back, bend down, grab hold of the leg to be shod, bend it back, and pull it up between his legs so he could see the full circumference of the sole of that foot. He'd study it for a beat or two, then, releasing the animal's leg, he'd go over to the rods of metal, shining as they hung there waiting to fulfil their purpose and be turned into horses' shoes. Next, the horse's front leg between his legs, his face facing towards his arse, leg bent up with his hands, Séan would hand me the small nippers to start clearing mud out from under the nail. This took strong, hard strokes, especially if you were handling the leg as well – which I seldom did, as it was just too hard for me. When all the mud, all the dirt and clay were loosened out, I would brush it away with a small, strong brush. I would brush and brush until it was smooth enough to receive its new, red-hot shoe.

The first time he corrected my Kerry accent, I had been mortified. But slowly, over time, I realized that not only had he spotted my great secret but he was actually helping me with it. He was the only one who knew. No one knew in Dublin or Gneeveguilla. No one knew, therefore no one knew or saw how important it was to me. Either way, he just joined in, and by now, many summers later, it wasn't really a game. It was just a thing between us that we both liked.

I loved the Kerry accent. It was colourful and musical and *so* much more interesting than the uptight dry sound of a Dublin accent. I loved *his* Kerry brogue above them all. More music. Softer. He'd roar out laughing when I asked him to repeat something.

''Tis my brogue you want to hear?' he'd say shyly.

'Of course it is,' I would fly back at him. 'Sure aren't you the only person in the whole of Gneeveguilla, even as far as Rathmore, who has even the slightest notion of how hard I'm trying to get the Kerry brogue right?'

This used to make him blush and smile together, which suddenly transformed his face into movie-star good looks. His free, clear laughter a soundtrack to an imagined movie called *Time with Séan*. I can hear it now as I write. It's seventy years later, but his laughter is still as young and fresh as the first time I heard it.

Grass

I would pluck a single blade of grass, then flip onto my back and lie on the green grass of a Kerry field. There were so many different greens there. So many different smells.

I would hold the blade above me. Rich green against ceramic blue. The beautiful design: the smooth curve rising from the rough base to the sweetly tipped top where the sides came together to form a perfect blade.

I would rub it on my hand and it would paint my skin green. I would rub it on my cheek and feel a shiver down my spine.

I would squeeze it gently, breaking the almost invisible pods, releasing tiny drops of slime, bringing out that potent, magic smell of grass.

I would rub the blade across my face and just lie there replete, exhausted and on a high. Most importantly, I was content: a happy city child lying in the middle of a country field drowning in the sunshine of a Kerry summer day. I felt a sense of freedom that seems impossible today.

I didn't know it at the time, but the memory of those days, when I was alone, happy, and completely free and safe would often save my sanity in the troubled times that lay ahead, like the days when I would have to walk down Oxford Street in London, tears of homesickness falling freely down my face for anyone to see. Sometimes I thought my heart would just crack with homesickness.

Homesickness is a sudden, private, potent thing, powerful enough to bring you to your knees. It goes as quickly as it comes.

The physical part of longing for the beauty of those days and that place still lives with me; it's alive and well and well protected in my mind.

Séamus S

Des would come to collect me from the RTÉ repertory studios on Henry Street when I was acting in plays there, aged about eight. One day, just as we were about to leave, I wanted to introduce my friend Séamus S to Des. Des and Séamus S already knew each other slightly from the canteen at RTÉ.

'Daddy, Séamus S says I'm very good at acting! He says he can teach me how different acting is with microphones!'

'Brenda is very promising,' Séamus S said to Des, with a smile. 'And I'd like to help her, if you think it's a good idea.'

'Can I, Daddy?'

I loved spending time with all the adult actors, and I really liked Séamus S, who spoke to children the way he spoke to everyone – giving them all his attention and making them feel that he was genuinely interested in everything they had to say. I found Séamus S fascinating in general. He was tall and quite elegant, always wearing white shirts that he had professionally pressed because he was a bachelor and had no wife at home to do that sort of thing for him.

Des did not seem very interested in Séamus S's offer, but when I got home and told Bina, she jumped at it.

'He said that you are very good?' she said. 'That's great.'

Shortly after that, my private elocution lessons with Séamus S started in his big house on Orwell Road, which happened to be right next door to the school where my mother taught.

Des led me up the garden path to where Séamus was waiting; Bina had phoned to arrange the time. They exchanged a few words, and then Des handed me over, telling me to be good, and that he would be back in a few hours to collect me. Séamus and I stood on the front doorstep together and waved as Des crunched down the gravel path, out of the gate, and into the car. We looked at each other for a few moments, and then we turned and he led me into the house.

The square hallway was bare and my footsteps were loud on the wood.

Is he too poor to buy carpets? I wondered.

Everything was bigger at Séamus's house than at mine; we had a narrow entrance hall, and his was a big, square room, very different from what we had at number thirty-four.

He brought me into the 'back room', which was very spacious, with big windows that were doors too, opening out onto what I could just make out was a garden. I couldn't see into the garden properly because he had heavy, dark red velvet curtains that went right down to the floor and they were opened just a crack, leaving the room quite dark.

There were lots of lovely lamps, all with red lampshades and low lights reflecting red everywhere. There were beautiful white fluffy rugs and two velvet armchairs and a velvet sofa in a silvery colour, arranged around the fireplace, into which an electric fire was tucked. There was a dark wooden table with books, pencils, paper, rubbers, and lots of board games arranged in neat piles. Folding doors, closed now, connected this room with the next. Against the wall, there was a small occasional table with a little pile of carefully ironed white handkerchiefs. I gasped as I took it all in. His house was gorgeous.

'Now,' said Séamus. 'Let's get you comfortable.'

Séamus's hands picked me up. He lifted me up in the air and sat me down in the middle of the enormous velvet sofa. We didn't have a sofa in our house, just armchairs, so this seemed very luxurious to me.

'How's that?' he said. 'I made some lovely treats, especially for you. You stay there, and I will bring them.'

The feeling of the soft velvet on my legs was wonderful. As soon as Séamus had left the room, I pulled down my knickers because I was dying to feel the velvet on my bum. It was lovely. I wiggled my bottom against the velvet until I heard him coming back, when I quickly pulled my knickers up again.

Séamus came into the room, carrying a large plate of little chocolate cakes. The cakes looked very pretty against the white-and-blue floral design of the plate.

'I baked these myself,' Séamus said proudly. His eyes smiled at me from behind his Arthur Miller glasses.

Séamus handed the heavy oval plate to me, and I took it in both hands.

His first gift to me.

My hands wobbled, and I dropped the plate, which smashed to bits when it hit the floor, scattering shards of pottery and pieces of chocolate cake everywhere.

I flinched and cowered back against the sofa, expecting him to shout at me and slap me.

'Oopsy-daisy!' said Séamus. He laughed out loud, enjoying my childish clumsiness.

'Don't worry,' he said, reassuring me. 'It doesn't matter at all. I have lots of other plates.'

Séamus got a new plate, and new cakes, and quickly tidied up the mess. Then, to my delight, he put on some music – he had a big wood-panelled record player and a collection of records – and we started to have fun.

*

Over the weeks and months that followed, every new experience I had with Séamus was wonderful: the music, the books, the conversation, and the gradually dawning knowledge that he really was interested in me and what I had to say. He read to me from books like *The Scarlet Pimpernel* and *Great Expectations*, grown-up books that challenged my mind and stimulated my curiosity, and that we could talk about together. He listened to my questions and answered them. He always taught me a poem, or at least a verse or two, before I went home.

Wonderful also were the experiences I did not have with him: the absence of punishment for having fun; not being hit and blamed; the absence of threat. I had felt cared for that first day when he picked me up in his arms and placed me on the sofa, and I always loved to feel his interest in me, knowing that he was listening to the things I said, answering my questions the way my father never did. He smiled at me, played with me, and asked me questions that made me think. He made everything so much fun, I didn't even realize how much I was learning. It was all perfect and just what I wanted. If anyone had suggested that I stay away from Séamus, I would have been furious. I felt very protective of the new world we were creating together: a world in which I felt cherished and in control. It was my special world that nobody knew about but us.

When I got home, Bina would ask me what I had learned that day, and I would recite the poem that I had recited for Séamus a few hours before. She was delighted that, under his tutelage, I was blossoming.

Shortly after we had finished recording eight plays by new Irish writers at the RTÉ studios – with me playing the child roles – he asked me to come over on a warm, balmy Sunday afternoon to talk about the work we had done. We were sitting on folding deckchairs – wooden frames with striped canvas – while Séamus read to me from *Moby Dick*. The garden was beautiful: a long rectangular space with carefully cut lawns and herbaceous borders filled with plants and flowers. Séamus told me that a gardener came once a month to keep everything looking nice. My legs were swinging to and fro over the grass as I listened to his calm, gentle voice narrate the story. I was happy.

As always, his voice soothed me into a doze. It was so peaceful that when he suddenly jumped up, saying that someone was looking over his garden wall and we had to go inside, I was taken aback.

I thought that I should fold the deckchair before going in, but this was proving very difficult; I sensed him standing close behind me. He reached his arms around my body as he bent over me to help. I wondered at his hands against the wooden frame. They were beautiful. His hand touched my arm and slowly stroked it. It should have tickled, but it thrilled me.

Séamus bent and kissed the golden hair on my arm. In that moment, I knew that something had changed. I felt my face flush red and couldn't speak.

Séamus stepped back and looked down at me from his great height.

'You're lovely, so very lovely,' he said. 'I love you.'

Nobody had ever told me that before.

I felt a surge of excitement as he leaned down and put his thirty-year-old lips gently onto my eight-year-old lips. He loved me! I felt a great wave of love and I wept. Happiness like this was not like the happiness I felt when I climbed a tree, won a race, or ate an ice cream. It was all-encompassing. For an hour or two, I didn't know what to do.

A few hours later, I looked over at Séamus. He smiled the special smile that told me he understood. He understood my tears; he understood my bright red cheeks. I knew that he did really love me, like no one else ever had.

It was 1953, I was eight, and I was snuggled up on the velvet couch, with Séamus nearby in his armchair, as we watched the news together. We often watched the news together, and afterwards he would ask me questions about what was going on in the world, to make sure that I understood and to encourage me to think. Learning from him was so much more interesting than learning anywhere else.

Today, the whole world was celebrating Edmund Hillary's feat of reaching the summit of Mount Everest. On the screen, the team looked haunted.

Séamus, who always explained everything to me, was explaining the epic climb now. He had got up from his armchair and jumped up and down.

'The Sherpas are the *real* heroes,' he said. 'They are the ones who braved the mountain first, preparing routes for Hillary. He wouldn't have been able to do anything without them.'

Hillary, who looked like death – he was a tall, painfully thin man with a lined face and sunken eyes – was being interviewed by a BBC reporter. The reporter had a strong English accent. Séamus started prancing around the room, mimicking all of the men on the screen so well that I slapped my hands on my thighs with laughter, and then jumped up and started jumping behind him. He could always make me laugh as nobody else could. He was witty and a brilliant mimic, well known for his impersonations. He could impersonate anyone: Churchill, Stalin, Charlie Chaplin, the man next door, the postman, and even me.

I knew how much Séamus loved to make me laugh. He couldn't get enough of it.

'Your laughter always stays with me,' he said. 'It stays here in the walls when you have gone.'

Nobody had ever said anything like that to me before, and I knew that it meant that he really loved me. That he was my best friend.

Then I saw him check his watch. This was the sign, our sign, that I had come to know and expect. Des would be picking me up in an hour or so, so time was running out. I knew what he wanted.

'Stand still!' I said.

He did.

I went back to the sofa and spread my legs as wide as I possibly could, my school skirt hitched up above my knees. This drove him crazy, as it always did. His hands darted straight into his pockets. I could see him fiddling with his penis through the fabric, stroking it and making it bigger. As he stared at the spot between my legs, I had an incredible feeling of power over him. I felt as though I owned him and I knew how he liked it when I bossed him around.

'You're so beautiful,' Séamus whispered hoarsely. 'Looking at your legs spread out like that drives me wild.'

I looked back at him and could see that he meant every word.

'Spread more,' he begged. 'Please.'

I had learned to love it when Séamus begged me for something that only I could give him, so I made him beg until he began to shake.

'You're driving me insane!' he cried, 'and I know that you have more for me. I'm yours. You know that. You're the only one.' His voice was very urgent now: 'Come on, come on! Do our secret, Brenda. Show me our secret. Please ...'

So I did.

I leaned back on my elbows and pushed my hips up into the air towards his face, letting my school skirt fall back. Then, with my right hand, I pulled the gusset of my knickers halfway across, showing him just enough. This made him gasp out loud, as if in pain. He fumbled with his belt until his trousers and underwear fell quietly to the floor, where they pooled around his ankles.

He grabbed his penis in both hands and pumped it up and down. He pumped and pumped to make it bigger and bigger until it was huge and hard and extraordinary looking. Now that he could see our secret, he pumped himself into a frenzy. He moved his body back and forth, pumping himself much faster now. He started to groan like a dying dog, he closed his eyes, and his face took on that far-away expression that told me the end was coming.

Séamus pointed his penis at my fresh, pink child's flesh until he screamed my name out loud as his semen spurted. It burst and spluttered out and arced through the air, spilling all around his groin and down his tummy and changing the smell of the living room. It went everywhere, and as it did, he moaned and groaned and whispered to me through gritted teeth, 'That's all for you, Brenda. It's all for you. All this is just for you.'

I was riveted by it. I was repulsed by it. I knew that it gave me power over him, and I wanted it for that reason alone. I understood that these parts of my body belonged to Séamus and nobody else, and that this was our secret.

After a short, tense silence, Séamus started to breathe normally again and the atmosphere in the room changed once more. When he nodded at me, I knew that this was my cue to bring two of the beautiful white silken handkerchiefs from the pile on the table behind the door. He was once more firmly in control of the situation, and I reverted to being his loyal subject.

I handed the handkerchiefs to him, and he unfolded one and wiped himself. He never let me touch him. He handed one to me, and I kneeled at his feet and wiped his semen carefully off his shoes and off the carpet.

When we had finished cleaning up, and Séamus had rearranged his clothing, we went together into the garden to that murky place beside the bins. There, we enacted the next part of our ritual.

Séamus handed me a box of matches. He held the handkerchiefs up between us while I struck a match and set them on fire. They burned quickly. He held them till they burned his fingers. Then he let them go. We watched them as they fluttered down. The ashes mixed with the mud beneath our feet.

This ritual complete, the mood changed as we went back indoors and into the big hallway, at a speed that surprised me. Des would be here shortly.

Séamus held my hand as we walked back to that wide, square hallway. I loved the feeling of his hand holding mine. My father, who had beautiful hands, never held my hand like that. Sometimes, when Des sat in his chair reading – holding his book with his left hand and elegantly smoking a cigarette with his right – I would long to touch his hands and feel his skin. It never happened, which made Séamus's touch even more important.

Séamus dropped his long body down and kneeled before me, just as I had kneeled before him minutes earlier. He threw his arms around my head and draped my school scarf snugly around my neck. I loved it; I loved it when his face touched my golden curls. It made me giggle, which made him laugh as he helped me to put on my school blazer, one arm at a time. Then he stood behind me and helped me to put my satchel on my back.

Minutes before Des knocked on the door, Séamus sprayed me with a sweet, sickly perfume, which he kept in the small downstairs toilet for this purpose.

'Why are you putting the perfume on me?' I once asked him.

Séamus leaned down and whispered in my ear.

'The car is small. The smell of sex is pungent, and one your father might identify.'

This relationship, the most important one at that time in my life, was conducted entirely in Séamus S's back room. For years, I only ever saw that room, the downstairs loo, and very occasionally the garden. The back room was our private world, our special place.

Looking back, it is hard to believe that we were able to keep our secret so easily, and for so long. It helped that I was already very good at lying. I had learned from my mother how to lie from an early age. I was regularly amazed by how easily people swallowed lies: big lies and small lies; big people and small people. Whenever a lie was called for, I lied through my teeth. I enjoyed lying to people because it gave me a sense of power.

Before ever I met Séamus, I had learned that my mother was the most difficult person to lie to. As she was so good at it herself, it was tough to get one past her. When I did, I would run upstairs and jump up and down, squealing with delight that I had 'got' her. By learning how to lie to my mother, I became skilled at it. It was routine for me to lie about almost everything. I lied to anyone who asked me a question I didn't want to answer. I lied if I was just too lazy to bother listening. I lied if I was bored. I lied just for fun.

Then I lied about Séamus.

While many people reading this will dismiss Séamus S simply as an abuser, I cannot think of him in that way, because I loved him, and because so many of the happiest hours of my childhood were spent with him. I understood that our secret was the price I had to pay for the deep friendship that we shared, and how much I learned from him, and I accepted this.

It was a deal that I had made. The price was high, but I was prepared to pay it.

Ena Mary Burke

Although she was already tall, she wore high heels. Proper high, like women-in-films high. I never saw her without a hat, always with a front net that fell to just above her eyebrows, which were perched just above a pair of quizzical bright blue eyes. She wore tight skirts. Proper tight, like women-in-films tight, with soft knitted twinsets. A ring of pearls around her neck, a silver watch upon her wrist. Though she was in her sixties, her back was straight and her legs were strong. She was a healthy, elegant woman who could transfix you by simply opening her mouth and saying 'Hello'. Her voice was like dark chocolate mixed with liquid gold. It fell around you like a velvet cloak. It made you calm enough to listen and brave enough to speak. It altered you in some internal way. It changed for evermore the way you heard or listened to the world.

Miss Ena Burke. The woman who changed me. I became her pupil when I was aged between five and seven; I'm not sure of the exact date. I am almost eighty as I write and I still feel her influence every day. She was the woman who impressed me more than anyone or anything in my life.

That was her game, of course. Changing kids. Opening their eyes and ears to this to that and that to this. To things they thought they understood. She took us all across the shapes and slants and sounds of language. She transformed my life and gave me one so different from the one I knew. So different from the one I had at home. So different from the one I had at school. So different from the world of all of them that here I am, many decades later, talking of the way she took my life and moulded it with rhyme and sound, with cadences and silences that allowed me to step into the world and let me earn my daily bread by doing the very things she taught me about.

Where would I be if Ena Burke, *Miss* Ena Burke, had passed me by? What if we'd never met at all? I dare not think. I let her down a time or two. But there she was and here she is, guiding me to write for you, the reader of these words. I write to tell my tale in hopes of entertaining you. Writing words, the things she loved.

Her temple, the place of learning, the stairs you climbed with relish and excitement, was 20 Kildare Street, in the centre of Dublin. Among my closest friends, or those of them who are left, is the Burkey gang. As I write I've just had lunch with my oldest, dearest friend, Anne Mulligan, who has come over from New York to celebrate with me and our friend Barbara Lyle that we've all survived, made it to the age of eighty. Barbara's memory of Burkey is of her saying, 'It may be spelled "any" but it's pronounced "eny".' We laughed, although part of me wanted to slap her face and point out how Burkey was so very much more than an elocution teacher. My memories of her include understanding iambic pentameter, aged eight, and being able to speak it with so much enjoyment that I'd almost burst. She'd give us great chunks of Shakespeare to learn, which we all did eagerly, and she opened up our hungry minds to the pure joy of language. I cannot even come close to describing what she gave me. From the darkness of Annaville Park to the bright, shiny room in Kildare Street, full of happy kids in the flush of pleasure that a good teacher can give. Yes, she fed me joy in those few hours on a Saturday morning – joy that I could easily tap into throughout the week. She was a mystery. An enigma.

There was no age limit for Burkey's students, which was good news, and delightful for me as I would always tag along with Gránia and her friends. She was smiling at us, waiting to guide us. And then she spoke!

She taught us how to listen. She taught us how to hear. She taught us how to touch that natural music that thrives within all kids, to reach the music deep within us and speak it out into the world. It is a love that's natural to children, a love of their own language. I'm Irish, so my first language is – or should be? – Irish Gaelic. But, in fact, English is the language I speak. There is a long chapter of Irish–English history that explains why that is so, which I'm going to avoid completely.

English grammar, composition, pronounced speech: all that was pretty boring to me. Then Miss Burke asked us to read out loud. Anything: that morning's newspaper, the first book on the shelf, the book in your pocket. Just read out loud. If you have never done this – *seriously* done this – I suggest you try. Open a book and read a line out loud. It's startling to hear your own voice for the first time. I am talking about a time that was on the cusp of massive progress in the field of sound. Go back even ten years and the difference is amazing. Go back sixty or seventy years; it is extraordinary to hear recorded sound from that time. Hearing your own voice is no novelty now, just as having your photo taken is, it would seem, a daily event for the young.

So you'd read.

The large first-floor room in 20 Kildare Street was of Georgian proportions, already over a century old, and the acoustics were wonderful. There were about twelve or fourteen of us in the class. I remember that one of the students was a funny girl called Gabrielle who worked in Clery's on

O'Connell Street, which must have made her sixteen at least. Memory makes her older. She was a bright spark. Her plain features were forgotten within seconds of talking to her, so engaging was her personality. She went on to become an air hostess on Aer Lingus long-distance flights. This, back then, was the most glamorous job in Ireland. It was a great occasion for any family with a car to fill it full and drive out to the airport to cram onto the tiny balcony (made famous when it was photographed defying gravity, as too many people, crammed dangerously tight, leaned forward as one to see the Beatles walk down the steps of their aeroplane).

Burkey would sit us down and got us to hold out our hands, palms down, and then she put on some fast jazz and got us to beat out the rhythm by slapping our hands upon our thighs like Sal Mineo, tom-tom style. This was hysterical for us, as we beat out rhythms to all kinds of music, from classical to pop. This happened every Saturday. She would end the class by sending us out onto Kildare Street with rhythm and music and poetry filling our happy little heads.

Then, one day, she suddenly sat us down, a serious expression on her face. This was so exciting in itself we were pulling at each other's arms and wondering in loud whispers about what was going to happen next. We all sat in a circle on the floor and watched her stretch up and take down a huge book from the many huge books she had on the surrounding shelves. Then she walked to her beautiful antique chair and, in one smooth movement, she tightened her tight shirt even tighter, crossed her elegant legs effortlessly, and sat down. As she gently crossed one delicate ankle over another, she straightened her already straight back. She straightened the book on her knees too, carefully turning over a page or two and, in the tone of voice that priests use for private prayer, she introduced us all to William Shakespeare.

I can hear her now, see her, revere her, love her, but more

than this I can thank her – *truly* thank her – for giving me the best of everything I have, not least the type of education and inspiration she provided. Every Saturday morning for years. Tears fill my eyes as I recall all the journeys of discovery she brought us on in that room above the garage on Kildare Street.

My closest friends – those of us who are left – are her survivors.

We all met there. Those of us who fell into the arts – directors, writers, costume designers, actors – all did very well in life. We went our different ways along the same path. I am still the only Irish woman to win an Oscar. Joan Bergin is a three-time Emmy winner. We all came through as a result of Ena's teaching.

The Battle of the Brogue

My friend Liz found a little, well-worn cut-out newspaper photograph of me the other day. We giggled as we read the faded print.

I was ten years old in the photograph. A pretty little girl. I was laughing happily, telling Liz all about the embroidery on the cardigan I was wearing that day. But she wasn't laughing or listening. She had her eyes close to the paper, squinting because she'd forgotten her glasses again. Just as I was about to reprimand her, she held her index finger up in the air as if testing the wind and whispered, 'Shsh,' so I held my whisht.

Slowly, Liz turned her face to mine with an expression of disbelief.

'Did you really do that?' she whispered.

'Do what?' I asked, grabbing the piece of newspaper from her hand.

I looked at the picture again. I looked happy in the photograph. *Had that been a truth day or a pretend day?* I wondered as I read the caption, which said I was a ten-year-old little girl who had just won a competition. First place for writing a play called *The Battle of the Brogue*.

Like a slap across the face, I suddenly remembered every detail of the whole episode, despite not having thought of it even once in over sixty years. Flabbergasted, I slowly sat down.

'Yes, I did do that,' I gasped at Liz. 'And it was put on for a week in the church hall in Milltown.'

We stared at the photo together in silence. Then Liz leapt up, saying that she was late to pick her grandson up from school. A barren woman, I sadly have no such chores, so I lay down on my bed and let my mind go back all those years, enjoying the bit of warmth I felt about myself. Indeed, after several glasses of red lemonade and a handful of custard cream biscuits, I was feeling so proud of myself you'd think I had won the Nobel Prize in Literature.

I remembered showing my script to Gránia. She – as usual, without consulting me – brought it in to Burkey. Burkey, against all the odds, actually liked it. All the fury and em-barrassment I felt slid away when Burkey decided we'd do our own production of it there in the hall in Milltown for the parents at Christmas.

I cast everybody in the class. A woman my mother knew made costumes. The story was about a country boy from Kerry who came to Dublin and was slaughtered for his Kerry brogue. There was a big scene in it about his shoes, which were also his *brógaí* in Irish and a sort of battle between the Dublin accent and the Kerry dialect. It was the only time I've ever used a pun and it was received by an audience I remember as rapturous.

The Mortification of the Flesh

Bina loved teaching, and her pupils were so fond of her they often visited us, even in the summer. She also had a good circle of close women friends – my best friend, Anne, was a daughter of Bina's closest friend, Mona Mulligan.

But when there was nobody visiting, Bina could be mercilessly violent. One of the worst things about her rage was its unpredictability. Sometimes we were punished for minor misdemeanours. At other times, we were very bold and received no punishment at all. The only constant was the shame we felt. Des, as always, remained detached from it all.

My mother was attracted to the rites and rituals of the Irish faith, especially the opulence and sensuality of Benediction. There was a man called Matt Talbot, who interested me. I read about him and the agonies he went through, torturing and wounding himself, all as offerings to God. When he died, they'd discovered that his body was wrapped in twine and covered in wounds. Reading about him really upset me, but I immediately identified with him, and instantly decided I too would wound myself and cut myself in order to be like him. So I wrapped thin twine around my waist until it hurt and wore it under my clothes until I bled. I thought that this meant I was sure to get to heaven. Even Bina was upset when I fainted and the family discovered what I had been doing.

Matt Talbot was never made a saint. When I was a kid, we all talked about it. Why not, if he was as holy and pious as everyone said? I knew he wore chains around his waist, offering up the extreme pain for the body of Christ. I thought this was amazing. I was infatuated by him. I knew I was going to be struck down for my sins, my many, many sins. I was terrified of everything because I knew I'd never get to heaven. Purgatory sounded terrifying. Would the beatings Bina gave me keep me safe, cleanse me, in some way? Maybe that was why she beat me, to help me into heaven. Gránia was the good one. She was brave. She had courage against anything that threatened her. She was always in trouble for it. Always. She was expelled from four schools in Dublin for things that would now be seen as signs that she was just a very bright kid who maybe should have been moved up a class. I used to put my arms around her when I felt she was troubled, lying on the uneven old mattress in the front bedroom, the room we always ran to for cover. The room where she let me see all her fears, the depth of her terrible anger at the world. Hate was her reserve energy, whereas I had no energy at all. Nor was I interested in finding any through something as strenuous as hatred or anger. Those little gems lived in comfortable sections of my head, fully alert and ready to burst into action when needed. Mortification called for different ingredients, different methods. Self-denial of some favourite food always impressed my mother, a bit more of washing of my own clothes and hoovering worked too. But was God really fooled by such nonsense offerings? Was he really impressed by something like the mortification of the flesh, which we were all told was a wonderful thing to do, one of the best ways of offering something up to Him? Unlike God, we were not just soul but body too. Flesh and blood. My guess was he would not be impressed by these offerings, maybe wouldn't even understand them. Without a body, not being made of flesh and blood, what could He know of human pain? But what the hell? I was alive, and the only person *I* had to impress was my bloody mother. That same mother was, of course, the best liar I knew. For example, once or twice during all those years of beatings, my father noticed a trickle of blood still fresh on my right calf, where she had beaten me with one of her favourite thorny branches.

'What's that?' he asked.

But before I had even taken a breath to answer she had jumped up, talking loudly, pushing my body to a different angle, shouting through a pretended laugh: 'Hockey,' she said. 'They played hockey today, and some awful girl whacked her on the leg.'

And Des – the fool – believed her, not seeing the craving on my face for him to ask the question of me, not her.

'But I don't play sports,' I could have said. 'Don't you remember? Visits to the convent? Forms you have to sign?'

My face heated slowly at the mortification that after all those weeks of talks and fights, the decision to let me not play sports for one year was completely wasted, but still served my mother's lies from time to time as to how blood came to be on my legs. I ached to tell him the truth, but would I have the nerve to tell *her*? I doubted it then and I doubt it now, so he never heard the truth. I guess there was terrible shame there, but not one I could use to offer God. I read somewhere, 'A moral is as a bullet in a poet's heart; a deadly wisdom.' I understand that now. I was not degrading myself to get brownie points from God himself, but from my mother. Maybe I could turn them around. I could fool my mother easily, but not God. So, in my continuing quest for mortification I suddenly remembered all those sheets of brown paper and rolls of thin twine under the stairs, used mainly for posting parcels of our clothes down to Gneeveguilla. Knowing immediately what to do, I slid down the stairs on my bum and pulled out a half-used roll of very thin, very dark brown twine. Just what I needed. I ran back upstairs and into the bathroom. This was the only room with a lock. Then, pulling the twine out at great length, as I pulled off my school uniform, then my vest and knickers, I tried to secure the twine around my waist. This took ages, but finally I found a knot that tightened it. I then did the same thing again, and again, and again until I could feel it cutting into my skin.

Great, I thought. *That should keep me out of hell at least.*

I leaned on the bath, dragging the thin twine as tight as was humanly possible and as tight as I thought suitable to sail through the pearly gates, giving the finger to Bina Murphy, who had been told by God to turn left five or six white ladders down. By 10 p.m., I thought I was going to die. I wasn't at all confident that what I was feeling mentally or physically had the slightest thing to do with Mr Talbot's Mortification of the Flesh, and feared that my death would be in vain.

Confession

I was in the church in Dundrum, all dressed up because I was going to confession. There were very few people there, three or four others and now me. I was trying desperately to think of something I'd done wrong. Had I committed any sin? Disobeyed my parents? Stolen something?

Suddenly it was my turn. I kneeled down and the priest pulled back the little purple curtain.

'Bless you, my child. What are your sins?'

'I haven't got any sins.'

'You must have some.'

'No, I haven't done anything.'

'You must have done *something* wrong,' he almost shouted at me.

Why was he annoyed with me? I couldn't understand it. I knew somehow that I was right and he was wrong.

I walked quietly out of the confession box. Out of the church. Out of the Church. I never went back again.

Fly-fishing

How can I write about fly-fishing when a winner of the Nobel Prize for Literature has already written about it so beautifully? His two lines say it all:

And the down turn of his wrist
When the flies drop in the stream –

That's it. There's really no more to say. But I can't resist writing about my father's fishing. He'd take his rod and, with the downward turn of his wrist, gently drop one of the home-made flies onto the surface of the water, thus beginning the repeated ritual of casting.

I love fishing because Des was a fisherman of lakes and rivers, a fly-fisherman, and he was very good. The fishing references in poems and novels spoke to me from about the age of eight.

That simple, quiet movement of casting is, in itself, pure grace to me. Some fishermen or fisherwomen never achieve it, and few are born with the natural talent to do it. I believe that my father *was* born with that gift. So beautiful was his casting that other fishermen would quietly lay down their own rods just to watch the graceful movement that Yeats wrote about.

My father and his good friend Johnson Purcell owned a small stretch of the River Suir, where it ran through Kilsheelan village in County Tipperary. They were both well-respected fishermen and it was wonderful to be around them. I showed an interest in all of it and quickly learned that fishermen are the best possible company for a child, because you aren't a child when you are with them. They included me in every single conversation. The technical stuff about fishing went over my head for years, but it was marvellous to sit squeezed in between three or four of Dad's fishermen friends on the vast sofa Johnson had in his spacious kitchen in his enormous house, and to listen to the love in their voices when the conversation mellowed into the actual lingo of fishing: the 'hooking', 'the bite', the 'reeling in', the 'letting out'.

By the age of nine or ten, my interest had grown deeper. I never saw more than four men fish that stretch of river and I saw beauty in all of them. I never saw a female anywhere around, other than me. Des saw my fascination with the art of it and got me involved in the tying of his flies. I felt honoured, and couldn't speak a word when I stood beside him in the small bedroom in Annaville. Des used to screw a little vice onto the windowsill and carefully lay down the three shiny metal boxes – one the size of a matchbox, one the size of a shoe box, and a magnificent silver one, oblong, about ten inches by five.

This last was the magical one. It had a tiny suitcase-style lever to open it. I always did this very carefully, because it was like stroking silk. And I did it in slow motion because it revealed the smallest, most beautiful, silver tweezers I had ever seen. They were held into the inside of the roof by a magnet. In the main body of the box there were two rows of small, see-through little boxes, ten in each row. Each of these was opened by the touch of a tiny spring so delicate that if you sneezed the whole lot would probably burst open together, silently revealing the coloured strands of silk – darkest black, whitest white,

Brenda's Dad, Des.

scarlet red, sun-kissed gold, deep-sea blue – all nestling tidily and curled up neatly, waiting to be plucked out with the tiny tweezers. The whole thing reeked of love and care and something else I couldn't understand.

Des had opened the smaller box to take out tiny strips of black wire. He carefully slid them into the vice and then whipped the weighted handle around a couple of times until he was certain he had a grip. From his small book-stand – it was always there – he had taken down a tiny volume, about the size of my communion missal, and very carefully turned the loose pages, stroking them into place lest they fall out. He opened it to small, see-through pages that were not pages at all. They were flat see-through pouches, each containing a perfect handmade fishing fly. I never saw him touch one; he'd just hold it up to the light to examine it. Des had started this collection as a boy. One day, while fishing on the Liffey, he'd met a fisherman called Rudy who must have seen the passion in the boy. Rudy had befriended him and taught him how to properly fish, to proper fly-fish. This was the man who had given him the bible-book. In the first half of that book there were drawings in charcoal. They were mathematical in their precision, every feather acting as a map of the anatomy of that particular fly. But when you opened the centre page an attack of bright colours hit your eyes, hot flames of colour burst into your face: the reds, the blues, the yellow-greens and golds. They devoured you, causing you to gasp in wonder at the glory of these tiny, small, feathered animals.

'Why don't you Sellotape them together?' I asked, but the words hadn't left my lips when I blushed red at how crass and awful the suggestion had been. He never gave dirty looks – that was Bina's speciality – but he did stop whistling, which was worse. I was utterly mortified.

'How many will you do today?' I asked.

He just smiled, looking at me, and said: 'I've no idea, Brenda.'

His answer was good. It said he had forgiven me, and soon he was whistling again.

Des and I could happily make an afternoon fly by by making flies, me using the tiny tweezers to pick out whatever colour of embroidery thread he'd ask for, and then watching in awe as his hands moved quickly and quietly, pulling threads and wires together into a bundle of colour that matched perfectly the picture in the little fly bible. They were luscious but they were lethal. All they did was act as bait. They were a trap, a beautiful, deadly trap, making the hook beneath, which would eventually lock on to some silver fish's mouth, the first step towards its death.

Fishing 2

He called me, smiling. I ran along the wet riverbank, skidding to the perfect spot in front of him with the usual beam of adoration on my face. He put his hands firmly on my shoulders, turned my body around until I faced the river, and then drew it back against his own. Then he astonished me by gently putting both his arms around me and sliding them slowly down my own young arms while taking my hands in his. He put his lips against my ear and said the words I had waited years to hear: 'Today I'm going to teach you how to cast.'

My legs began to wobble, my bladder almost leaked, and I could feel tears pushing behind my eyes bursting to get out but *no!* I must *not* do that.

I rubbed an arm across my nose saying, 'I'll get the flies. The priest. The nets. The lot. Hang on, hang on!'

Still trying to keep the tears back and snots away, I reached into his fishing bag, taking all the things he'd need and gently, calmly, laying them down in the right order in a straight line along the pale green Tipperary grass.

He brought the rod high up across my head from his right shoulder, where he carried it like a soldier marching with his gun when he wasn't using it, bringing it down with his beautiful hands, and, taking my own small hands, he curled them gently around the base of the lighter rod he'd chosen. Together, we slowly moved it up into the air. To do this, Dad had to hug the whole of me. As we bent over to reach a full-length cast, his whole body was leaning against mine, making me feel that I was suddenly in heaven. I was dizzy with delight at the physicality of it all. This man. This father. This seriously untactile man was hugging my whole body against his and gently – ever so gently – his hands were guiding mine to help me catch a fish. Was that the most beautiful thing of all? His magnificent hands holding both of mine around the rod? It was certainly the most intimate thing I'd ever experienced with him. I thought I would die from the love I had for him. I felt it then and I feel it now. Somehow, he made me feel that I was doing this completely on my own, causing the whole of me to float somewhere just above the ground. To feel what I would come to know as ecstasy at the perfection of it all. Pleasure and terror at the proximity of his body against mine coupled with the massive compliment of actually being allowed to touch one of his rods.

Everything about fly-fishing, from making the flies, to choosing the rod, to casting your line, to hooking a fish, to landing it on to the riverbank. Everything is beautiful. Peaceful. Graceful. Skilful. Mesmerizing …

… But then comes the kill. The actual killing of the fish right there on the riverbank. I have never been able to watch it, never mind do it.

A fish can't scream, nor do they have a hoof to kick you. They have no bark, no hiss, no sound at all. A landed fish twists and squirms in obvious distress. Its gills closing down, stifling it to death. Feeling just as it would for us if we humans were drowning. Not a quick death. We knew that, so someone would always be ready with a thick piece of wood about twelve inches long. While expertly holding the arse-end of the fish, they'd bash it on the head with one ferocious blow, causing blood and brains to dribble out of its dying mouth and its beautiful silver body to grotesquely flounder, jump up and down in a last attempt to survive. Some elegance in the final, ugly, jerky moves of death. There's an irony in this. They call the thick, heavy wooden murder weapon a 'priest'. I don't watch this now. I did once. I ended up in a bush as sick as a dog, vomiting up the trout I'd eaten earlier for lunch.

I was super-aware of how alive Des was when fishing. All the shyness, the antisocial tendencies, the disbelief in himself, the arrogance, the lack of any physical affection for any human being, the snobbery: all of these unpleasant traits seemed to disappear when he was fishing on a riverbank.

Many years later, when we had a little boat, and a little house in Connemara, I met and become involved with a beautiful man called Joe Pilkington, and all of us would go out onto Lough Corrib for a day's fishing. I was always sharply on my toes on these beautiful days. I was keen to remember every detail I'd learned as a child. Usually I did. They regarded me as a decent fisherman. For a woman.

Writing About My Father

Why now? Writing about my father? I have been doing that for weeks now. The usual stuff. You try. You get a good line or two, but you have to open up the memories. Memories I would never have opened if I hadn't chosen to write this book. Memories that were happily tucked away and are now being forcibly dragged out, spitting straight into my face, mocking every word I write and screaming 'false' at me.

The Island

Joe and I grabbed the food satchel and a few extra flies and lines while Des waited in the car for us. All his gear was in the boot so we could set up on the lake's edge and silently perform the preparatory rituals for a day's fly-fishing on a sparkling Lough Corrib. There was total silence while Joe worked on the little outboard engine and I threw in the raincoats, listening to the soft purr of the small engine that was a musical accompaniment to the quiet movement of the boat leaving the land. We would glide around the lake, both men's eyes fixed in concentration as they watched for that tiny movement of a fish grabbing at a fly. Then, how accurately they moved the boat towards that spot. Suddenly I would notice that the engine had been cut off and hear the sweet whistling of fishing lines being swirled in circles high in the air, landing their well-crafted bait onto the tiny circles in the water with the accuracy of a 180 score in a darts match. There was tense, perfect silence as they reeled in their lines slowly, smoothly, hopefully. No luck? Childish curses of frustration as they laughed and swished their lines up in the air to cast again. Sometimes, I would take my own rod and join in but, more often than not, I would move to the rear of the boat, stretch my legs out, lean back, and just watch them fish.

It is hard to explain perfection. But even as I write, I feel the pleasure of those days. Sitting in a boat on the magnificent Lough Corrib, breathing in the clean Connemara air, and watching the two men I loved most in the world doing something they were both so good at. That perfection sat quietly between the three of us: Joe and Des and me.

They were so alike, yet so unalike. They were good together. They were good apart. They were the best of friends in that magnificent way that men can be friends with men in a way that women can never be friends with women, not in the depth or intensity of the love nor in all the attending that comes with it. It's because of sports, I think: men were in sports teams. They played sports. Talked about sports. Admired each other's prowess. It started when they were boys, made it easier for them to find common interests. Girls didn't have the same thing, or not in the same way. A girl at that time kicking a ball in the garden would usually be told to stop, come in, help her mother. We never had as much time to spend with our peers just having fun, sharing a common interest. Men's friendships always seem deeper to me, and I believe that's one of the reasons why.

Watching these two men fishing together and seeing the love between them, entwined with their love for me, was so powerful that sometimes I cried tears of happiness. Whenever they witnessed this, they would laugh aloud, saying, 'We love you too.'

If things were slow, they would fire the engine up and head for one of the hundreds of tiny islands on the lake. We would kill the engine, jump out and haul the boat up to settle safely on the sand. We would empty out the well-worn fishing satchels and Des and I would go gathering twigs and broken branches so that Joe could perform his magic and light a fire.

I have no idea how it is done – God knows I have tried – but Joe would lean down, rub twigs together, blow like hell, and then call out, 'Fire! Fire!' as he grabbed the empty kettle, ran to the lake's edge, filled it up, ran back, and placed it carefully on the fire that Des and I had been coaxing and that was now a decent yellow flame.

I still have the kettle. It's so hard to describe it, this sacred kettle. I got it from the kitchen and am looking at it right now. I want you to see it through my words but now, as I write, suddenly, I do not want to talk about the bloody kettle at all. My heart has started pounding and, instead, I desperately want to put my arms around those two beautiful men and kiss them until they know – at last – how deeply I loved them both, in very different ways but with equal passion.

What wouldn't I give for just five minutes from that time. To reach across. To live five more minutes with them, completely free and unaware of the tragedy that would separate us far sooner than life should ever kill a thing of such beauty.

Kay's Death

We were upstairs, playing Ludo, when we heard Bina come in from shopping. The usual sounds: sighing while she hung her coat on the creaky coat hanger in the hall, the rustling of the wrapping paper.

(The rustle reminded me to ask if she had remembered to get me a few sheets of butcher's paper from Dermot the butcher; he couldn't understand my love of butcher's paper but, from time to time, he would reluctantly hand over a few sheets, looking at me as though I were mental. I loved it, because you could slide your hand across one side and it was soft. The feel of the paper pleased me. This touching of paper became a lifelong habit, causing trouble and embarrassment in stationery shops from Dublin to New York to Sydney. It was one of the things my husband, Barry, would love about me throughout our marriage.)

Suddenly, Gránia nudged me out of my daydreaming.

'It's too quiet downstairs,' she whispered.

I held my breath and listened. Not a sound.

'What's she doing?' Gránia asked, questioning the sudden break in busy scurrying that usually accompanied the unpacking of shopping.

We tiptoed out onto the landing and sat on the top step of

the stairs, listening. The top step of the stairs was our only source of information.

'She's on the phone,' Gránia deduced.

'What? Why?' I asked. 'I didn't hear it ringing.'

'She must have phoned someone.'

This was very unusual. The phone was a magical thing. We were the only people on the road to have one. In general, if you wanted to make a call, you went to one of the public phone boxes on the street, where it cost four pennies, but because Des was a journalist in the *Irish Times*, he'd been given one to use whenever the paper needed to contact him. It was something of a social coup, and Bina made the most of it. It was quite funny how her accent veered towards posh when 'our phone' came up in conversation. She had bought a really beautiful little table for it, and a square of white crochet to put under it, and had put one of my school exercise books and a pencil beside it to write down messages and phone numbers. Behind it was the biggest book I had ever seen. Des had explained that this was a 'telephone directory', in which every phone number in Ireland was listed. Gránia and I were forbidden to go anywhere near this altar in the corner. We knew that Bina was nervous of it too, so for her to be on it now, this early in the morning, with the door closed, was a serious matter.

As we craned our necks, we could just about hear her saying quietly, 'Of course I will. I'll phone you back tonight. If you need anything, Des can drop me over later. Okay so. We'll come over tomorrow. Goodbye now, and may God bless you in this time of trouble.'

Frightened both by the words and the tone, our bodies tensed as we waited for her to come out. Then she opened the door of the front room, so slowly it put us both on edge. Her body emerged, hands holding her face as she raised it to the ceiling, stifling the smallest cry of pain, which cut through me like a knife. Was she laughing? Coughing? No, she was weeping into her hands. Instinctively, we ran down the stairs to comfort her, although we weren't too sure how to do it. Then she sat down on the stairs. Now she was holding her head, crying only to herself. I was consumed with fear and love. Gránia was whispering gently to her, consoling her. Suddenly, Bina moved even closer to Gránia and put her arms around her waist, mumbling into her clothes, saying she was sorry, saying this was a tragedy.

I looked over at Gránia, whose face was as white as a sheet.

'What's wrong, Mammy?' Gránia asked. 'What's wrong? Has something happened to Daddy?'

Oh, my God, Jesus. I let out a noise that made Bina think I was choking.

'Daddy is dead! Daddy is dead!' I screamed. I grabbed Bina's arm. I hugged her as tight as I could. I was bawling now, terrified I would hear the words, 'Your father is dead.'

'Did he crash the car?' I screamed.

'Daddy's dead!' I screamed again. 'Daddy's dead. Des is dead.'

Bina turned and slapped my face so hard that my feet left the ground. I felt and heard my head crack into the wall. Blood began trickling down the back of my nose, making me swallow some before the rest burst out and down along my face. Afraid to speak, I curled quietly onto the floor, making sure I was out of reach. I watched as Bina put her hands, ever so gently, on either side of Gránia's head. She gently brought Gránia's face across until it was a few inches from her own face and, in a voice breaking with sadness, looking straight into her daughter's eyes, she said: 'I'm so sorry, Gránia, but Kay Geddess died last night.'

'Kay Geddess did what?' Gránia asked in a flat voice.

'She died last night.'

Gránia's body fell to the floor. *Has she died now?* I asked myself. But she got to her knees and bent over, laying her head on Bina's lap. I can still see us all in that knot at the bottom of the stairs. Bina stroked her head as one would stroke a cat. Slowly, the words were sinking in. Kay dead? It must be a mistake. You went through dying before being dead, and Kay had not been dying at that hockey match last week. She had played a game of hockey against us, in fact. She had come back here for a glass of orange juice. Kay was a loud, happy girl with a permanently flushed face and a wild, thick head of reddish-blonde hair, always braided by her mother into two thick plaits every morning. She was tall, gangly, and popular. She was head girl in her school, and sports captain too. Kay and Gránia were inseparable. Kay lived in a huge house on Ailesbury Road. They were the only really rich people in our world and they were as exotic as all get out. They threw parties for no reason, wild parties at which we were allowed to run around the place, completely free. But *dead*? Our dog, Buster, had died. That was all I knew about death, apart from Jesus, who had died for me.

Gránia stood up. She walked over to the window and just stood there, staring at nothing. Then she reached down, grasped my hand, and pulled me up beside her. She lifted her dress, spat on her hem the way Bina did on her handkerchief, and started to clean up the blood on my face. I could hear her heart beating.

'It's okay,' Gránia said. 'Try not to cry. Death comes to us all. We know that. Sometimes it takes children. I don't know why. Why Kay? We'll never know.'

Bina sat on the other chair, weeping away on her own. Gránia took my hand and brought me upstairs into the bathroom to wash my face properly. She got a clean facecloth out of the hot press, ran it under the hot tap, and rubbed it so hard around my face I thought my skin was going to tear off. She was looking through me and was mumbling to herself in such a low tone I couldn't catch it all. The word 'why' was there a lot. As her scrubbing hardened, her personal monologue stopped and she lay the flannel across the bath.

'Guard the door,' she said, as we walked into the front bedroom together. She closed the door. Suddenly, feeling as strong as Superman, I leaned against the door, ready to hold the fort against anyone trying to enter and disturb my sister.

The muffled sound was confusing until it got a little louder. Gránia was crying. I was afraid and in shock, not knowing whether to hold my back against the door or run over and hug her. Gránia never cried. I couldn't remember ever seeing her cry, not even when she stood in front of me and took the blows Bina meant for me. Never a tear. There were times I would watch her face fire red from the beatings, but she never gave in. I think she did it to outwit Bina. To stand and take it until Bina exhausted herself and had to stop. But now Gránia's friend had *died*. How? She had been in this very room, alive, on Friday. Now it was Monday. It couldn't have been anything like a car crash or Bina would have mentioned it.

We must have stayed up there for hours. Bina didn't order us downstairs once. Suddenly, I felt real sorrow for her and an awful fear overpowered me again. Deserting Gránia, I opened the door and tore down the stairs to find Bina. She was in the kitchen, staring out of the window. I ran at her body, grabbed her thighs, rubbed my face on her stained apron, and screamed into it: 'Don't die, Mammy. Please don't die. Please, *please* don't die. Will I die soon? How did Kay die?'

Things moved in a slow haze that night. Des drove Bina over to Kay's house, leaving us a little lost. He came back alone. He sat into his chair, picked up his book, and bent his head to read. Why, oh why, didn't he give me what I needed? I wanted to be held by him. Be comforted by him. To have this foreign thing explained. A child dying? Old people die, not children. *I'm* a child. Jesus, could I just die tomorrow? Right now?

I sat in the chair beside Des.

'How did Kay die?' I asked.

Des placed his finger on the line he was reading, looked up, and said, 'She died of TB.'

'What's that?'

'An infection in the lungs.'

'Does it hurt?'

'Not much.'

'Was she sick last Friday, when she was here?'

'Yes.'

'But she looked well!'

'I know.'

Des lifted his finger and continued to read.

Angry now, I screamed into his face: 'I don't understand how she died so quickly!'

Des looked up again. Putting a bookmark in his book, signalling he was going to speak to me, he did. He looked straight at me with his clear blue eyes, which were, unusually, sad.

'Do you remember when Kay went to stay with her Auntie Bridie in London a few years ago?'

'Oh, yes.'

'Well, the truth is she didn't go to London. She actually went to a special hospital called a sanatorium where they treat only tuberculosis, TB. She was there for four months and then released, as she had improved so much.'

'So why has she died?'

'Well, obviously, she wasn't cured. It is a real tragedy, Brenda. For her family and friends and, of course, for your sister. I overheard her crying in the bathroom.'

How did I miss that? She must have sneaked out. Poor Gránia. The thought of her crying in the bathroom for Kay brought me a new level of pain. I was ignorant, insensitive, and selfish. I had let Gránia down. She who protected me, fought for me, laughed with me, laughed *at* me with tangible affection.

Brenda's parents, Des and Bina, as middle-aged adults.

I ran away from Des and up the stairs to Gránia, who was sitting on the bed, brushing her hair in what looked like slow motion. I felt so heartbroken for her. I sat on the bed beside her, took the brush from her, and slowly, gently combed her dull, straight hair as if it was delicate gossamer. She leaned her head back, closed her eyes, and allowed tears to fall slowly down her cheeks. Even today, this is the only clear image of sorrow I carry with me.

The next day was rushed. Tears blurred the ironing of clean blouses, the taking out of the good coats, hats, shiny shoes. We needed good clothes for the viewing. What was that?

Hundreds of people came to Kay's funeral, all of them devastated. Kay was laid out in her coffin with her hair perfectly set and a ribbon holding it in place. She looked as though she was alive, but at the same time she was more still than anything I had ever seen before. Too small to see Kay properly, I pulled myself up by the edge of the coffin to peer at Kay's dead face. I put my hand in and touched Kay's cold fingers.

I can see now that this was the beginning of my fascination with death and dying.

Mary Lavin's Car

One of the girls I was sort of pals with at the Loreto College in St Stephen's Green was Mary Lavin's daughter. Mary Lavin was already a very successful writer and hers was the only family I knew who lived in a flat, rather than a boring house like mine. Mary's Morris Minor was bright green and you could roll the roof back, turning it into a convertible, so exotic that we would all flush, stutter, and start to jump in the back whenever she started to roll up the soft top.

'Thanks!' I would stammer whenever she said, 'Hop in, Brenda. I'll take you home.'

Whenever this happened we all became serious show-offs. We'd lean right back, letting the wind blow through our long hair, thinking that we were movie stars. Marilyn Monroe or Rita Hayworth or some other actor we had seen in the local cinema.

If you had told me then that, one day, I would drive down Hollywood Boulevard in a Mustang convertible doing exactly the same thing, I would have been worried for your sanity.

The First Cut

Concentrating on the blue veins under the thin white skin on the upturned wrist of my left arm, I took the little silver blade I had stolen out of Des's safety razor and dragged it gently back and forth across them.

I held it between thumb and index finger. Moved my arm back and forth to get the weight of it. I was astonished that something so lethal could weigh so little.

Everyone was out, so I knew I was safe for at least an hour. My legs were a little shaky, so I moved over and sat on the side of the bath, bright sunlight shining through the window behind me.

I held the blade up to the light and the sun flashed on the silver-blue metal. It mesmerized me. I brought it down flat against my wrist. Cold metal on angry skin. It soothed me. I adjusted my grip a little until the weight felt right.

I held my breath. Steadied myself to do what I had spent a year planning. I lifted my right hand and, without hesitation, slashed the blade down hard, breaking open the skin on the inside of my left wrist. I gasped as I watched the first drops of red blood spill out of me and dribble into my palm. Like a snake, I struck and licked it up with my child's pink tongue, and as I swallowed it I almost fainted. The salty, dirty taste of the blood was beautiful! I instantly wanted more, so I squeezed again … harder, to push more blood out.

I bit my lips to trap the noises in my mouth. Pleasure? Pain?

My throat seized up as more red drops slid out along my skin.

I had never had power over anything in my life. People who feel powerless will do things to make them feel powerful. I had done just that. I now had power: over my own life, over pain; but much more important than any of that, I had power over my own death.

I kissed the red snail trail and took a white towel to press against the wound. A dark red stain spread across the whiteness and a bright new smile spread across my face. The towel was just like the loin cloth on the body of Christ in the crucifixion. It was full of blood, that picture, and it was everywhere. There were three in my house alone, and dozens of them in Gneeveguilla. I liked that picture. I used to study it at Mass in Kerry. Our pew was right beside a sculpture of it and it was absolutely terrifying – the big holes in his hands from the brutally big nails they had used to nail him to the wood, blood from both hands pouring down, dripping, his feet crossed one over the other, only one nail for them … Lots of blood, though. They must have run out of nails by the time they got to his feet. That must have really hurt and it had caused buckets of blood to fall in rivers to the ground. There was a huge stab wound below his heart – a spear, they said – and there were streams of blood pouring out of that too.

I moved the blade away and looked down at my wrist. A thread-thin line from side to side marked my first scar. I was impatient now. I would have to wait a day, probably two, to do another cut, taste more blood.

I knew these scars would be the first of many more to come. My thirst for death was fit and strong, my appetite for secrets growing.

My guile was good as I pulled my cardigan sleeve down to hide the work I had done. A beautiful, bloody secret settled on me. I had found a different road to happiness on a gorgeous sunny day in Dublin town.

Up to the hardware store to buy a coupla one-sided blades. There were loads of places around the house small enough to hide them, even from Bina's eyes, which were all-seeing.

There'd been a row because I only came second in the Irish dancing competition in the Father Mathew Hall. She was stiff with anger. If looks could kill ...

So I pulled an easy trick out of my bag of weapons against these attacks and burst into a screaming fit of tears. I knew that if I screamed loud enough it would finally interrupt the calm and quiet my father commanded in order that he be allowed to read his books in peace. It always worked. He'd lift his head, put his finger on the word he was reading, look impatiently at me and ask: 'What the hell's going on? I can't concentrate on my book!'

His sacred books. When he was reading, we crept around the house, whispering. When he was in the back room writing, we crept around the house, whispering.

Sometimes he'd leave the door slightly ajar. I loved peeping in to watch him as he typed. He smiled a lot then. This was a rare thing too. I loved seeing it and it made me want to be exactly like him. In fact, when he was away I used to go in and play with the typewriter myself. I became good enough to get temporary secretarial jobs later on in life, typing for extraordinary people, when I needed a proper job to pay for my rent in London.

The Sight of Myself

The sight of myself in the mirror was the sight of a stranger. I loved the clean lines my father's razor made through the snow-white shaving foam around his jaw. It was obviously dangerous: how he used his hands to stretch the skin taut to take the sharpness of the blade. What if his hand slipped? Would I like that? Would I like to see his blood trickling red along the foam?

Those little blades were sharp. I had stolen one from the pretty box of six they came in, neatly wrapped in slightly oiled paper. They unwrapped silently and smoothly to reveal a blueish metal blade cut so fine and smooth on either side it made me gasp.

I took it carefully into my fingers, held it up to the window, and marvelled at its style, its form. So simple. So small. So lethal.

At the age of ten I began to buy them, as I've said, in hardware stores but also in chemists' here and there around the town. I would stash them, take them out, and stroke them.

Then, unexpectedly, the cutting had started. Paper first, then hair, and then my skin. Just little scrapes. Leaving marks. Visible, but barely.

I would make up stupid answers if I was questioned: How? How? Oh, bramble bushes. The cat. Whatever.

I would touch the scrapes under the table when we were eating. They calmed me. I owned them. Somehow they were suffering separately, yet with me. For sure, there was a love between us.

I hid my stash of razors behind the picture of the Infant of Prague that hung on the wall. Dead safe. My mother prayed to him. A fat baby with a silly hat on. He had magic powers like the rest of them she prayed to, but I felt somehow he'd quite enjoy this hiding lark. A bored, over-worshipped baby would just love the excitement and the disobedience to his God of hiding weapons of destruction under his silly hat because a ten-year-old kid was desperate to hide her secret.

Sick and Tired of Praying
(Infant of Prague)

Iwas sick and tired of praying kneeling down, elbows on a backward-turned chair, fingering beads while thanking God. I was being forced, now, to thank God – again – for everything, but I was afraid of everything, so why thank him? Or even pretend to like him? Anything he'd given me, I didn't ask for.

Bina pushed me, yet again, to join her on another of her damn novenas. I really didn't want to. All my life, it seemed, I had been falling on my knees and praying to Jesus. These obscene pictures were everywhere: on every wall, in every house, in every village on the island. Most of them were versions of that big stupid one, the Sacred Heart, where Jesus held his own heart, which was, for some mad reason, stuck to the outside of his chest, with his hands pulling back his loose robe so you couldn't miss the bloody organ. Mind you, there wasn't a spot of blood on his hands, only on the great nails that were used to fix him to the cross; there were trickles of blood dripping from them. He was doing this to atone for my sins, I was told, but it was all so out of proportion it was laughable.

There is blood everywhere in Catholic pictures and, although my love of blood was very alive in me, the amount of blood involved in them put me off as well as drawing me in. Did I begin my love affair with blood partly through these holy pictures?

This little guy from Prague – now where the hell was that? Near Lourdes? Fatima? And why did he have no blood on him at all? Not a drop! I had checked every inch of the picture in my bedroom. I guessed he didn't need gimmicks like that. He had won fans, hands down, with just the costume. His outfit was hilarious: a Renaissance white ruffled collar hung around his neck, under which was another collar attached to a cape of plush red velvet cloth, and underneath all that the cream-coloured nightdressy thing they all seemed to wear. On his head he had a thing the size of a bucket. It was shiny gold with tiny doors, like the entrances to a tiny cathedral. There was layer upon layer of small gold gargoyles, each more vulgar than the last, topped by what looked like a couple of upside-down broken eggs, dripping yellow yolks around his head. I think it was supposed to be his hair, sticking out from under that ridiculous crown. It was mad, but it made me smile. I felt almost sorry for him, overdressed like that. It reminded me of when my mother dressed me up in luscious clothes when we did the dreaded 'visiting' rounds.

Looking at him now, though, my feelings quickly returned to quite disliking him. I felt my body heating up. I finished off the rosary, kissed the beads, and dropped them in the bowl, where they lived with all the other magic relics Bina had gathered over the years. Bits of saints' corpses. A bit of skin. A bit of hair. And then her *coup de grâce*, the best catch of them all, a splinter from the cross that Jesus died on!

Furious at the whole insult of it, I stormed out and ran upstairs and into my bedroom. I slammed the door and fell onto the bed, tears of rage on my face. I had turned to blow my nose on the corner of the sheet when my eye caught the big picture on the wall. There he was again. The Infant of Prague.

Not even aware that I was doing it, I found myself pulling a chair over to the wall. I climbed onto it and leaned over, above the tiled mantelpiece, pressing my weight into my palms with a surprising sense of achievement. Leaning on my left arm, I reached my right hand up along the side of the picture. To my amazement, I reached much higher than I thought I could. The old wooden frame of the picture almost crumbled in my hand. How long had that picture been up there? I couldn't remember the room without it.

I had enjoyed him for a while. He used to comfort me, insofar as he was a kid, like me. There was a statue of him in Dundrum Church. I would kneel in the pew nearest to him and pray, and pray, and pray. Well, that's what people thought. In fact, I was working up my own relationship with him. It wasn't hard. After all he was, as I said, a child. The only one to speak for us other than that intolerable Baby Jesus. I loved his tiny, fat chubby hands and, when no one was looking, I could reach out and stroke them, transferring my dreadful deeds into them, begging forgiveness for being the boldest girl in Ireland. For wetting the bed. For telling lies. For looking out of the window while doing my homework. For running up the stairs instead of walking. Those tiny hands of his were magical, for sure. He was the only statue I took seriously. Was it because this Prague guy helped me, or was it his magnificent velvet cloak? The same red as the velvet one up in the Father Mathew Hall, where I took part in dancing competitions. Did I just associate it with success? Was that why I never doubted he'd heard me loud and clear, and believed me? Or was it because, unlike the Sacred Heart, there was no blood on him? Of course it was that.

I slapped the crumbling frame down onto the bed. It was picture-side down, with ancient, dirty brown paper holding the picture in place. There were rusty little clips along the side, so broken they fell out on their own. I turned it over and there we were, face to face. I felt fear for just a beat, but then it turned back to hate.

I left the picture on the bed and stared at it for long time. Stared and stared, until I felt tired. Then I lay back on the bed, trying to catch a thought that was niggling at the back of my mind. Something dark. I wasn't sure what was happening, but now I know what it was: a stirring in the depths of my soul, a dark movement that would live inside me for the rest of my life.

I sat up and then walked slowly over to the small dressing table. Among the mess I found a little pair of nail-scissors. I felt a sudden physical strength as I picked the picture up and walked slowly back around the bed. I stood for a while, staring at that faded picture of the Infant of Prague. I gazed at it for what seemed like hours, but was probably minutes. Then, gently, I picked the paper up and very, very carefully, I began to cut it.

I cut his little baby hands. I cut his little baby face. I cut his little baby legs. I cut his little baby ears. I cut his little baby toes. I cut his little baby eyes. I cut his little baby mouth. I cut his little baby neck. It was such a vicious and necessary act.

Irish Dancing

My Irish dancing teacher was Miss Boylan, who lived on the top of 11 Hume Street in Dublin, near St Stephen's Green. She taught dancing behind a little sweet shop on Aungier Street. I was a little doll, a friendly child and a very good dancer so I was allowed to visit her at home. Her brother lived up a tiny stair above her flat. He worked, Miss Boylan explained, for Jacob's biscuit factory and was allowed to bring all the broken biscuits he wanted home. I never saw him but I saw the bags of biscuits and got to eat some of them when Miss Boylan's sister Molly, who seemed to exist mostly for the dispensing of biscuits, put them out on a plate for us tiny dancers.

Book Hardware

I am addicted to hardware and paper shops and have been as long as I can remember. Barry, my husband, used to whisper to me, 'You're going to get arrested, Brenda! *Stop* stroking the fucking paper! You'll get arrested for being a perv!'

But there are far more jewels in a hardware shop than in a stationer's. A hardware shop is heaven! A cloud of ecstasy envelops me as I go through the door – any door of any hardware shop anywhere in the world. The sensations of my body quickly change. My heart beats faster. My breathing, faster. My hands sweating, my fingertips itching as I stroll between the shelves, the endless shelves, of shining nails, tools, screws, paints, brushes, buckets, mops, feeding troughs, farming spades, farming forks, spoons, knives and forks, batteries, lampshades and bulbs, rolls and rolls of wire, of twine, of chain, of cotton, each with its own measurements.

One day, as I was strolling in a hardware heaven, something silver caught my eye. It was a packet of little silver blades with one side blunt, the other sharp, a thick ridge joining them, supplying a solid, balanced 'thumb press' to safely use this tiny, dangerous tool. I *had* to buy a pack. A lightning rod of pressure moved my hand to pick one up. I felt strangely comforted.

I found my first shop in Rathmore. Was I seven? Eight? My timeline for this book is not good at all. I have laughed for it, I have wept for it, I have pop-slammed a lot of doors on good friends' efforts for it, but times won't add up for me. I have tested other people too, and found that it's quite normal for us to have vague, mixed-up ideas tucked away in an imperfect memory. Of all the people I asked, by far the most competent and interesting were policemen and teachers, which – when you consider it – makes sense. Policemen have to remember names, dates, colours, smells, visuals, facial features, speed, car recognition, car plate numbers, and on and on. Teachers' memories of the children they teach are just as clear. How about you? Can you reach back and remember, for example, what age you were when you had your tonsils out? For me, it was over seventy years ago and I was buying razors.

Hefty Hilda

She was a hefty girl with no humility and her name was Hilda. I must have been questioning something about myself because suddenly I blushed. There's no way Hilda could make me blush, yet she had made me blush so much that my face and neck were burning. I felt stupid, which I hated. Hilda had the advantage now, which I hated too. These were the times I wanted to just step aside. Not to hide, just not to be there for a while. My eyes get weary of seeing life and sometimes closing them doesn't work. Thinking hurts your eyes anyway.

You could turn and just walk away. I knew Hilda wouldn't even notice. I didn't want to hurt her, so I said, 'Let's walk.'

The impurity of those few words, I knew, would cost me. She had a grey bandana-like thing around her neck. It was unwashed, and her school blouse wasn't ironed properly. It never was. We all smirked about that every day, and we hurt her every day. We knew that we were hurting her but it never bothered any of us enough to stop.

She was the *fat girl* too, so we called her Hefty Hilda, knowing it would hurt her. I wanted to ask her why she never got angry, but I never found the time.

This time I had the time, so I was going to talk to her. Find out did we hurt her or, better still, was she even aware of what we were doing to her. I knew exactly what it was like to be hurt, so I would quickly spot if she was lying. I could swallow her if needs be. Cruelty came easily to me.

If she knows I know all about hurting, would she tell me her secret? Because she had a secret: survival. She did that with ease.

I couldn't handle it at all. I admired her in a roundabout way, even liked her. I protected her from the totally vicious red-headed Paula, who could kill you in a heartbeat with one sentence. She did it all the time, but by some miracle of life she liked me.

Hefty Hilda had what was called 'a crush' on me. That was gas. Some girl got a crush on you and suddenly became your slave.

I was very lucky indeed on this turf. I was quite exotic. When I was working on the radio, I got mornings off to wander through Dublin town, down to the GPO where all the drama was recorded. There I would spend the day with actors, big, bright, happy people who leaned over backwards to make you laugh. No pretend laughs there. Knicker-wetting clever fun was had. I think that was the first time I felt a sense of belonging.

They knew I wanted to be a boy. I think Hilda did too. This was probably why she had such a crush on me. It gave me power over her and allowed me to pull myself into another skin and wait for my slave.

Hilda had left a love letter in the pocket of my blazer that morning. A bad poem and I had told her so. This was probably why she was so down. I knew I had hurt her.

Later, in the cloakroom, we lay down, and resting my breasts against hers, we fell asleep. I didn't know it then but she would be the first of many women in whose arms I would happily fall asleep. There was a gentle sexiness about it, but I was using even that to hurt my Hefty Hilda.

But she was clever. We cheated at exams, coming second
– her – and third – me – out of a bright class of thirty-three
upper-middle-class girls. My coming third out of thirty-three
brought my mother real pleasure. She would run around
telling all her friends, who were genuinely delighted for her.
From time to time I felt a twinge of guilt, but I was willing to
ride high on the bits Hilda had managed to sneak over to me
during the exams.

Considering how little time I spent there, I did very well
at Loreto College, and still had the gall to bask in the glory
of someone else's hard work and someone else's good brain.
Hilda promoted herself into a sort of minder for me, protect-
ing me from the nastiest girls in school. She even brought in a
couple of cans of beer one day and we sneaked into the cloakroom and knocked them back. I got slightly drunk and decided
to kiss her on the lips. Maybe that was, in fact, the cruellest
way of hurting her.

She got me through so many exams in that first and second
year, but I was able to return the favour by helping her out
with Latin, which she hated and I adored, and algebra, which
I was good at too.

After leaving school, we completely lost touch. I wonder if
she's still alive somewhere, maybe with a lovely farm and lots
of children. She told me that was what she wanted.

Pink Witch

My fourteenth birthday was coming up. I had spent every day since my thirteenth birthday begging my parents for not just a new bike but for a Pink Witch bike. I had only ever actually seen one of these bicycles, as they were prohibitively expensive and hard to get.

But my fourteenth birthday came and – to my astonishment – there it was in the hallway, leaning against the wall with gaudy pink ribbons badly wrapped around it wherever possible and a massive birthday card sitting on the saddle.

I nearly broke my neck sliding down the stairs and running over to touch it. Was it real? Was I still asleep and dreaming? But no! I ripped off the gaudy wrapping and jumped up onto the saddle so I could ride it up and down the tiny hall. This was ridiculous, so I got off and opened the hall door, wheeled out my Witch, slammed the door, mounted my bike, and turned right at the garden gate to go to the top of Annaville Park in order to give me the longest virgin ride down to the main Dundrum Road. Just enough to test the tyres, the balance, the bell and all the rest of it.

At the top of the hill I stopped, got off, turned the bike around and remounted. Then, with all the concentration of a professional rider, I started pushing those pedals round and around as fast as I possibly could. My heart was thumping in my chest and I felt slightly sick with the excitement of it all. I built up speed and went hell for leather down towards the main road. I was flying!

When I turned to come back up the park I saw Des standing in the garden in his Foxford woollen dressing gown over his striped pyjamas. He had a camera in his hand and I heard him laughing as I whizzed past him. His laughter only added to my ecstasy as I did a skid-like turn, with one foot scraping on the ground for balance. I was very good and very confident on a bicycle. I still have the photograph Des took that day. The photograph of me on one of the happiest childhood days I can remember.

Des was pleased that I could ride so well. He had taught me how to do it. Before I ever touched a bike, he taught me about every inch of the machine. Why it was built that way. Its purpose. How each piece was connected to the next piece and why. The balance. I had learned everything I needed to know about a bicycle before ever getting on one.

Of course, the one thing that Des had failed to make clear was how, by gathering speed, the whole thing flew along, somehow staying upright and defying gravity by means of sheer unadulterated magic.

I came back in. Bina was washing the dishes. She was happy for me.

'Are you happy now?' she asked me. 'Are you? You've been tormenting me for a year to get you a Pink Witch and now you have one. Are you happy now?'

Bina was grinning from ear to ear. Seeing her happy made me almost unbearably happy too. She was lovely when she was happy. The whole house changed then. Even Des involved himself much more with everything.

'Yes, yes, yes!' I cried. 'I'm happier than I've ever been in my whole life! Thank you, thank you!'

Then I remembered all the sacrifices Bina had told me we would all have to make to get a Pink Witch. Everyone would suffer. I could forget any treats, money for liquorice pipes, for ice cream, for Cleeve's toffee bars ... I would have to go without *all these* if I was ever to get a Pink Witch. I had wanted that bike so much I had happily agreed to go without. But now I realized how much love it took to make sacrifices like that. I jumped up, threw my arms around Bina's neck, almost knocking down her light body, and hugged her till I thought she'd burst.

Thank you. Thank you. Thank you.

On that first day I went to get Anne Moran, who lived next door. I told her to get her bike out. Anne was busy, but she said she'd join me just before lunchtime and we'd go down to Bird Avenue to test drive my new bike. Bird Avenue is a wide, long avenue, perfect for bike-riding.

Des, who worked five days a week and was off for the weekend, was back sitting comfortably at the kitchen table with – as ever – a book leaning against the milk jug. He continued to read, drink his cup of tea, butter his toast, and turn a page without batting an eyelid. It was amazing how he could read anywhere. There was always a book in his left-hand jacket pocket and if he had five minutes to spare out it would come, a strip of paper torn from that morning's copy of the *Irish Times* marking the page. He'd read with a fierce concentration. Getting his head back up out of the book would require almost a shout straight into his ear.

Bina was ready to go. She wore a shabby coat and medium-high shoes that had seen better days, and she was carrying an old cotton shopping bag, but enthusiasm buzzed around her. She had to call into Clery's on O'Connell Street – the most magnificent shop in our world – and this was the cause of her excitement. Her mood was contagious, so both of us were high and happy as we set off down Annaville Park for her to catch the 48A bus into town. I waited with her till the bus came and then turned back up the park to wait for Anne.

Eventually, Anne came out on her two-year-old Raleigh bicycle, which all the other kids used to queue up to get a ride on or even clean for her. Suddenly it looked old and tired beside my new, sleek and shiny Pink Witch. I felt a little sorry for Anne, but had no intention of letting my sky-high happiness be reduced by her inferior transport.

Anne and I shouted joyously as we got to the end of the park, calling to each other the safety rules our parents had drilled into us for months and months. We were good kids and we followed the rules to the letter.

We turned right across the main road and settled into a cruising speed as we passed the Mental Criminal Hospital's massively high stone wall on our right, past Highfield Road on our left, past the three new shops on the right, and past Windy Arbour, after which there was a sharp right bringing us into Bird Avenue. But before turning there we had a dreadful fit of the giggles, which must have been brought on by the new bike and the fun of us riding together. In an exaggerated fashion, we indicated that we were turning right off the main road. The hilarity of it all made us fall off our bikes and roll around the footpath in delight.

Once we had calmed down, we sat on the pavement for a while having a serious conversation about school, boy crushes, and Anne's first period. Her period had arrived four or five months before and had scared her, as her parents had told her nothing about it. Neither had mine.

Even now, talking to Anne, I couldn't be nearly as open and honest about mine as she was about hers. I felt a kind of shame. I knew it was irrational and stupid, but I felt it anyway. Anne didn't. She loved the whole business of changing into a woman. She was so excited by it all. But surely being a woman was a hell of a lot more than just having periods? Séamus S had explained to me his experience of turning from boy to man, and it had been quite moving. I think that he had been very lonely through his teenage years. He had questioned me a lot after my first period arrived. Looking back now, I see that that this was around the time when he stopped doing anything sexual in front of me. I still visited him, I still enjoyed his company hugely, and he was still the only person who could make me laugh in a grown-up way. But nobody knew anything about *that*.

Suddenly not knowing what to say, I jumped up and grabbed my bike.

'Race you to the top of the avenue!' I said.

Anne and I cycled for an hour or so. How clearly I can remember the ecstasy of riding round on that magnificent pink bike: the world flying by, my hair blowing in the wind, and my body feeling totally in command of this beautiful machine.

Finally, aware that lunchtime had almost passed, we decided to head home and stay out of trouble. The road was free of traffic, so I increased my speed a little to catch up with Anne and pass her by. Getting ready to pass her and show off the superiority of my Witch, I looked behind me, looked in front of me, looked behind me again, and then pushed my right hand out as far as I could, signalling my intention to turn. Next I remember the thrill of standing up to get more pressure on the pedals and whizz past her, screaming with happiness.

No one knows exactly what happened next.

All I remember is lying on my back in a blazingly bright room with everyone in sight dressed in white as they drifted back and forth behind the man who was leaning over me, his nose almost touching mine, his breath against my cheek.

'I have to do this,' he whispered. 'It's going to hurt. I can't give you an anaesthetic because you're going in and out of consciousness, but if I don't do it now the lip tissue will start to knit and that could leave you with a harelip and we don't want that, now do we? So I'm going to cut off that piece of your upper lip that's hanging down and it'll all be grand. But this will hurt.'

I think I heard a scream. Or I remember a scream.

It was and is all a blur.

I remember waking in a bed. Not being able to move. I tried to turn my head. Nothing. My legs. Nothing. My arms, my shoulders, my toes, my knees. Nothing.

Petrified, I moved my eyes from side to side. They worked. I saw the hospital screens around me. I heard no noise at all. I knew where I was. But what had happened to me?

Now I screamed. Nurses came. Ordinary nurses and a few seniors, a sister. They hushed and whispered all around me, telling me to relax, that everything was all right.

'The doctor's on his way,' they whispered. 'He'll be here soon, Brenda.'

My mind was racing, but it was also empty of information about the last few hours of my life. I could feel the heavy flat weight of sheer panic. I broke into hysterical tears. Then, feeling the agony that crying caused as it shifted the skin around my face, I fell back in shock.

Now there was a cacophony of noises. The jarring sound of metal objects rattling against each other. Terrifying whispers. Whispers all around me. Pain everywhere. I clearly remember a doctor, probably in the accident department, saying that I was in and out of a coma. A harelip? Questions attacked me from every side. It seemed that I was the only one who didn't have a clue what the hell had happened to me.

'For God's sake,' I screamed, 'would someone tell me I'm not going to die?'

I had horrific injuries, on which doctors worked for nearly two years. One of my teeth was surgically removed from my ear. The only link to the outside world were the visits and letters from my family; Gránia wrote to me almost every day.

For Bina and Des, the financial burden of the hospital bills led to debts that they would be paying for the rest of their lives; it did not occur to anyone to sue the driver – who was Frank Aiken, minister for external affairs, one of the most famous politicians in the country and a close colleague of Éamon de Valera, or perhaps it was his son, we were never sure – until it was too late. My parents were in shock and would remain in shock for a couple of years. But at some point a tall young man came to visit, bearing a bunch of bananas. Someone introduced me to him as 'the man who knocked you down'. As the son of Frank Aiken. He said he was sorry. He left the bananas on the bedside locker. In those days it was easy to cover things up; the powerful were untouchable. A few quid to the guards might do it.

At home in bed one night, later on, Bina told me about how she'd been coming home from town, sitting upstairs on the 48A bus, when there had been a delay of about ten or fifteen minutes because of a crash in Windy Arbour. Everyone on the bus was gawking. A little girl, they said. Knocked down by a car. All the young shopper-women on the bus made the sign of the cross and offered a prayer for the mother of the child.

Bina had got off the bus at Annaville Park and walked up the road, her body bent from the weight of the two overflowing shopping bags. She walked with her eyes on the ground, her head thoughtfully tilted to one side. So vulnerable.

She didn't see the two young policemen standing on the front doorstep and, in her innocence, when she did see them had no idea in the world why they were there.

She invited them in, put down her shopping, and politely offered them a cup of tea. They declined, telling her that they were very sorry, but that they had some bad news for her.

I can't describe the rest of that day in my mother's life. The next-door neighbour, Mrs Harrison, told me years later that Bina became hysterical. She fainted several times.

'I saw it, I saw it!' she screamed. 'From the top of the bus, I saw it. That's my youngest daughter, Brenda.'

She'd screamed as she fell to her knees and all the strength left her body.

But one of the clearest memories I have from those two years is my father's first visit to me after he got back from Belgium, where he had gone to report on an international meeting of some sort. Suddenly, from nowhere, he was there at the end of my bed. He stared at me and froze. He gasped as he saw the ugly wooden frame around my face. The shiny silver screws screwed tightly into the four corners of the brace: the thing that had been made to hold my head together. He stood frozen at the end of the bed. He must have been like that for four or five minutes. Then his suitcase fell loudly to the floor as he ran around the bed, fell to his knees, and grabbed my hands, kissing them so hard I thought he'd further break my already broken fingers. He kissed and kissed my hands, moaning and muttering words I couldn't hear. He lifted his elbows up and leaned across to touch the timber brace around my head. He leaned in and kissed the little bits of skin that were not bandaged. He kissed them as if they were the most beautiful jewels on earth, whispering quietly to the both of us, 'God almighty, who did this to you? Who the hell did this to you?'

Then, in a shriek of pain that all the hospital could hear, he threw his head right back and screamed, 'Dear God – if there *is* a God – help me find the man who did this to my child.'

Shocked at his shouting, I cried.

I watched him drag himself together. He turned his head to look at me. He just stood there and stared at me. Stared and stared as tears of utter sadness rolled from his dark blue eyes down his beautiful, smooth-skinned face slowly all the way to the floor.

I had never seen him cry before.

I would never see him cry again.

Afterwards, although I was tired, I turned to Audrey Swann in the next bed. Audrey had burned herself badly when her nightdress caught fire. She had no skin left on her back at all and had already spent months lying face down. We were two broken girls. But I was glad Audrey was there. Despite the pain and fear, somehow we found things to laugh about.

Years later, in a grocery shop in Blackrock, a woman came up to me. She put her arms around me before I recognized her. She told me I looked great. We'd been oohing and aahing for a minute or two when I realized who she was: lovely Audrey.

Teeth

That fragment of time when your body is in the air, propelled by violence from one point to another, causing you to go face first through the windscreen of a car is indescribable. It ripped my face apart. Broke my nose. Broke my jawbone. Ripped one ear almost off my head. Broke both shoulders, both wrists, my left leg, a few fingers, a few toes, and ripped out all my teeth. My upper teeth. All broken into little bits. They went everywhere inside my mouth, outside my mouth, inches from my left eye. There were little shards embedded in my head, which made shaving it painful. It was a car crash that made people gasp in amazement that I was still alive. It was an accident that kept me in The Meath Hospital for almost two years. It was a car crash that took two years of my young life away from me. It was a car crash that locked me up in a hospital room from the age of fourteen to sixteen. It was a car crash to be referred to from then to now by my friends and family as The Accident. It was a car crash that would change me in every possible way for the rest of my life.

Insurance

I remember the police coming into the hospital. My mouth was stitched together and I could hardly speak, but they asked me questions. They were trying to get my side of the story. If what I said was the truth – and I had no reason to lie – then the accident was the fault of the driver, and not mine. I don't know exactly what happened but Aiken was the minister for external affairs, one of the most powerful politicians in Ireland, and it kept him safe from being accountable. There were many witnesses to the accident, which is how my parents knew that it hadn't been my fault. Perhaps they were all paid off too. I will never know. I'm sure the cops were in cahoots with the Aikens. That's the sort of thing that happened.

We should have been in line for an insurance payment but I never quite understood it until years later, when Gránia tried to make a claim on my behalf. She said we had missed the deadline by a week. People have asked why my parents never made a claim. All I can say is that people, even educated people, were very passive and fatalistic in the face of authority in those days. I don't think it ever even occurred to them. And you have to remember that bureaucracy was much harder back then. It was more difficult to find things out. Gránia's efforts came to nothing.

Years later I found myself in a room with Aiken's son. Bile rose up in my mouth. I turned around and walked out.

Hospital – Leaving the Meath

The ward was bustling with excitement. I was going home – finally – after almost two dreadful years in the Meath Hospital. Bits of me – arms and legs – in a cast. All of me in bed for those two years. The painful business of learning how to walk again. The nurses did all of it. The doctors came in once in a while and made pronouncements. They were like terrifying gods determining your fate.

Now I had been told I could go *home*.

I was actually *going home*.

I had been told about a week ago and I had been running around the hospital ever since, saying my farewells to all the lovely people who'd done their best to cheer me up when I was in a dark and painful place, praying to God to give me some relief and let me die.

No doctor had comforted me, ever. Those arrogant men I had grown to hate. They'd enter the ward dressed in civilian clothes. Smart suits, neat dark waistcoats. No white coats for them. White coats were for the minions, the flock of junior doctors who wore their white coats unbuttoned at the sides, flapping in the air as they ran behind the consultants looking like a flock of geese, wings fluttering in an attempt to fly away from these dreadful men, maybe to heal elsewhere.

I hated those senior doctors. They never spoke to me directly.

They spoke to their flock *about* me as if I were a damaged leg of lamb. I had no goodbye to say to them.

I ran down the long corridor to the cleaners' little tea-room – a hole in the wall, basically – to hold them and kiss them and thank them for their daily hello-how-are-yous, for the Crunchie bars they bought me out of the wages that barely covered their own grocery bills. I hugged and kissed them all.

I ran on down the stairs to the huge, steaming kitchen, looking for the women who cheered me up six times a day, every single day. Breakfast. Morning tea. Lunch. Afternoon tea. Dinner. A nightcap. When I couldn't lift a cup to my mouth because of my broken fingers, wrists, and arms, they'd gently lifted the pink plastic-spouted cup to my torn lips, which had so many stitches in them that you'd think a black spider was sleeping on my face. They'd find the hole through which the plastic straw would fit and they would feed me with love and laughter. I hugged and kissed the sweaty faces of the dinner ladies slaving over boiling saucepans, cooking something awful for the patients. Even as I hugged them tight with gratitude and love, the stench struck me and I realized that this was where these women spent hours and hours each day. Yet still they found it somewhere in themselves to cheer the patients up. Saints, all of them.

Now, two years later, officially better, I was becoming a showpiece. Bina was taking me everywhere, talking and talking about how all my facial scars had completely healed, which, to my surprise, they had. I guess being fourteen had helped. I have healed well ever since, and God knows I have needed to.

Damaged

I was so damaged. By illness. Isolation. Lack of education. Gránia saw all this. And I knew it. Knew too that she was the only person with the slightest interest in helping me. Des? Bina? In small, rather weak ways I've contemplated how this could happen. After all, she was a respected teacher and he was a successful journalist.

How did it happen?

How did they *let* it happen?

I still have a great mountain of resentment, embarrassment, anger, frustration at having had no organized education for years of my youth. Nobody picked up on it. I missed out. I was not given any foundation of loving to learn. Séamus S had picked up on it, and he taught me something every time I was with him. He really was the only person who understood me until decades later, when I met the man I married.

Lourdes

I remember people struggling to get the wheelchair onto the ferry to travel from Dublin to Holyhead, then onto a bus to drive to Dover, then onto a ferry to sail to France, and then onto a train to Lourdes. We stayed there, in a strange little flat, for one week.

I cannot even imagine what that journey must have been like for Bina. She was pushed and pulled around at every change of station on the journey. Having a wheelchair was a nightmare. Several times I got out so she could close up the chair and lift it, first high, in through the train door itself, then along the thin corridor, carriage after carriage, until we found the one that matched our tickets and fell into it red-faced, sweating, and exhausted. How the fuck did she do that? Yet I have no memory of tension at all. Nothing negative towards me, for once. Guilt?

I enjoyed the French trains. There were three-seater velvet benches facing each other. We were me, my mother, the person assigned to help my mother on the train, and another cripple, his father, and his father's helper. The helpers – of whom I saw very little – were in the carriage next door so the father, Mr Cafferty, quietly and solemnly helped lay out the grown-ups' luggage before setting out the kids' bags. He introduced himself formally: Peter and his young son, Eamonn.

Eamonn looked awful: hardly there at all. A bundle of flesh wrapped up in a woollen blanket. He had no arms, just little hands coming out of his shoulders. I don't think he had any legs. His head was fine, with perfect ears. His face was unblemished, a perfect nose. He had great teeth in a perfect mouth that was quick to smile and quick to laugh, as I'd find out again and again as we tumbled along our pilgrimage route to holy Lourdes.

As travellers sometimes do, we ignored each other for the first hour or so. The carriage we were in was big with a wide window, through which you could see right across the landscape as we flew along through the French countryside.

I felt great freedom. But I had a problem. My attire, in which I would be spending twenty-four-hour stretches, was awful: a longish nightdress, a shroud, with no sleeves. My legs were covered yet easily accessible for inspection, injections, resealing of the dressing on the right and a wipe-down on the plaster of Paris on the left, and so on. Although I was well used to it all, I didn't see why I couldn't wear one of my own pretty dresses instead of this too long, too big, dull, dull garment.

Our lovely neighbour, Mrs Harrison, had made me a practical long cotton dress for my trip. A bit *too* long according to the rule book for Lourdes we'd been sent months ago. I'd been playing in the front garden when she held out her Protestant hands and gave it to Bina. She looked confused as she parted with it, in its expertly wrapped pink tissue paper with a tiny pink bow pinned on, turning it into an obvious gift. She really had a special touch. But she was puzzled by this Catholic carry-on.

'You're going to France, Mrs Fricker?'

(The women on our road never addressed each other by their Christian names.)

'I am, Mrs Harrison.'

'To get a miracle for Brenda?'

'Oh yes, Mrs Harrison.'

'Mmm ... do you think it will work?'

'Oh, it will,' Bina enthused. 'Catholics just go to Lourdes and pray. We pray to a girl called Bernadette. A little French girl. A dead girl who Our Blessed Lady appeared to a hundred years ago. Sick and crippled people have been going there ever since. They go in droves from all over the world. And yes, Mrs Harrison, there *are* miracles. In the grotto where she appeared there are hundreds of pairs of crutches hanging from the rock where they were hung after the people using them just got up and walked without them.'

Mrs Harrison looked slightly sceptical. Bina was hurt and angry at this heathen questioning of the miracles.

'I'll take a photograph of them,' Bina said. 'Des got me a little Brownie camera for the trip, so yes, we'll take a photo of those crutches for you, so. I'm certainly praying for a full miracle for her and that she'll be able to leave her crutches behind too. But if that doesn't happen, she'll be blessed by so many priests, she'll attend so many religious ceremonies – especially the candlelight one where, I'm told, a lot of miracles happen. There'll be masses, benedictions, prayers, and ceremonies that will change her for ever for the better. I know this in my heart, Mrs Harrison. But if she doesn't receive a full miracle cure it will still have a profound effect on her, which will comfort her enormously and might help with sleep, depression, loneliness, amongst other things. No, Mrs Harrison, I'm sure this trip will ease some of my little girl's pain.'

Aaggh, aaggh.

She whispered my name as she stumbled onto Mrs Harrison's shoulder. Mrs Harrison slowly put her arms around her and called her husband's name. Within seconds he was at her side. She leaned over and kissed his cheek while whispering to bring

Bina into their kitchen. He took Bina in hand as if she were a tiny bird. He took her small hand with his big, hard-working Protestant hand, and guided her around the bush and into their Protestant kitchen where he gently sat her down, handing her a beautifully ironed tea towel to wipe her face.

I'd followed Mrs Harrison into her Protestant kitchen and, though worried about Bina, I was deadly curious about this Protestant room. I swallowed hard against a strange, sweet smell. Was that what Protestants smelled like? Did they have their own special Protestant soap? I noticed that everything was ultra-neat and tidy. I'd heard about how Protestants were like that.

He put his two big Protestant arms around the women, who were both crying now, and rocked them a little in a comforting way before bringing us drinks of water in the cleanest, most beautiful glasses I'd ever seen. Kindnesses I've never forgotten.

How pitiful and sad we must have looked. A broken hunch of holy folk, bright-eyed in their belief that in this foreign place – where they spoke a foreign tongue, and where a little girl broke down, went mad, and told a long, long tale of things she saw or thought she saw while lying in the grass – I would be healed.

*

The hotel in Lourdes was gorgeous. Sparse. A tidy bed. A tiny table. Nicer than the ward for sure but still …

I missed the ward. I'd been there so long. My home from home. While Bina unpacked our bags I peeled myself out of the wheelchair and sat on the side of the bed to smell the fresh French air. Then I panicked, stood up, and walked, clinging to the high walls of this beautiful old room. They were higher than I'd ever seen at home other than in very old houses in Dublin. I felt lost, threatened, and afraid. We were told little beyond what we saw. Was this where I'd be turned into a miracle girl?

No. There were the Baths, the famous Baths. Of course I'd heard amazing things about them. *Scary* things. The Baths and the big main grotto where the cures happened. I'd heard how there'd be screams like from a mad house, screams of disbelief and shock at actually seeing a miracle happen. It must be terrifying.

Not knowing I'd fallen asleep, I woke to find Bina at the table reading a huge book. *The Bible*, I thought as I sat down to taste the awful tea, the foul-smelling milk, and the bitter biscuits for the first and last time.

And once again, without any warning, I felt a surge of love for her. How desperate her need was. How desperate her belief in this holy place, belief that it would give her back her old life where I was well and life was good. She saw clearly what she'd had and desperately wanted it back.

For the first time I saw the guilt, the mountain of guilt she was carrying. For buying the bike at all. For letting me ride it on the main road. For everything. I noticed new lines on her face as she drew her tired hand across it to wipe the murky sweat away. *How dreadful this must be for her.* How alone she must feel.

Where was Des? He should be here. The physicality of it all was draining her and all the way during that long, long journey she'd had to depend upon the kindness of strangers to haul me on and off trains and boats and cars, to hold my forehead as I constantly threw up. The physicality of different motions, including the need to hug me when I cried out in pain. The terror of what my life was and where my life was going. Being dragged around like this was scaring me.

I knew I could show her that I knew her suffering. All the time from leaving hospital to getting here we'd protected each other. Somehow we'd sheltered each other from the real darkness of it all, and we were only able to do that because in some odd, twisted way we loved each other. I – and she

I'm sure – never felt that love again in any active way, but we did then.

The big book turned out to be a guidebook. We were given this to read before starting any treatments. The big book turned out to have lots of contradictions.

But so what? I thought. They have to guide us, and we have to trust them and …

I felt her try to touch the edge of me. To touch my being, my ghost, my body and my soul. And still I felt remote from her.

A maid brought in some food. I was trying to remember how to say 'thank you' in French when I saw Bina putting her hand in her pocket and giving coins to the girl. And then it hit me that *all this time* Bina had been speaking French!

'Where did you learn French?' I asked.

She threw her head back and laughed so loud it shocked me. She laughed again. No madness there. She roared aloud. Some madness there. A sound I'd never heard before. A sound I'd never hear again. She blew her nose and then she coughed. She crossed the room and took the food and laid it out before me.

I slept again and woke at ten. The room was busy, Marie – the girl we'd been given to assist us in Lourdes – buzzing about. This time she had assistance from a gorgeous young man. I envied him his strength.

This was the third morning of our visit. The time was flying. Bina was so happy. She understood the vast number of schedules that were brought to us every evening. Today she told me there'd be four Masses. The first two to be held in a nearby church, the second two to be held in an older church beside the Baths. Marie was mumbling what I guessed were prayers as she glided around the room. She ironed my shroud, she laid out my shoes and socks, and nodded to my mother, expecting songs of praise, which my mother duly gave her. Delighted now, she left the room, telling me she'd be back at four to bring me to the Baths.

There'd be four masses before the Baths. Those words again. The Baths THE BATHS THE BATHS. The words were on everybody's lips, whispered fearfully and far too reverently. They caused great excitement, these Baths.

Lunch was served in a long bright-blue room with refectory-tables, with not enough room for the width of the average place setting. It was easy to feed me from a bowl held to my mouth, which Marie did with great humour. She was one of the happiest people I've ever known. Bina hated the food, she said. She just bought bars of chocolate and a loaf of white sliced bread and a lump of cheese.

After lunch, we piled into a bus specially designed for wheelchairs, stretchers and so on and were driven to a church just half a block away. We were walked carefully in and up to the altar. There wasn't one of us who could kneel. This was so immediately sad that I felt my own tears flowing. I didn't even bother trying to control them, because crying here was not a sin. I felt completely sad. A helpless sadness that anyone could be born legless, born armless, born sick.

Bina had taken her cardigan off. She was wearing a thin, pretty cotton dress, almost see-through in the evening light. Her dress had no sleeves. For the first time, I saw her naked, beautiful white arms, which must once have lovingly held my father's body close to hers.

She helped remove the clothes from my upper body and hung them on the wall. With the speed of light, to cover my nakedness, they put on a long, loose armless garment which fell to below my waist in the front and behind my knees at the back. The material just hung there. A helper gently washed my face, combed my hair, and moved me across to another queue. That queue was much longer so, embarrassing as I found it to be in the wheelchair, I was grateful for it now. I realized how sensible it was to just wheel everybody around. It was easier. They could line us up and move us from here to there.

We were in a huge hangar, all the cripples lined up against a back wall, with holy workers running back and forth. A few feet in front of me there were about ten open stalls made of cement bricks, waist high, like the ones we put the cattle into in Kerry in order to milk them. Two people guided you down the steps and dunked you, quickly and quite violently, right under the cold water. Then they pulled you out again and before you could catch your breath they scooped water into an enamel mug and made you drink it. This was bad enough, but what made it worse was that the man in front of me, whose back was covered in open sores, had been in thirty seconds before me.

Sloth

Guilty, m'lud. I'm described this way by others, and I agree. Throughout my life there have been descriptions of 'the sickly child in the back' or 'she's in the Meath again' or 'she's in hospital again'.

Today, I have no memory of ever being naturally energetic. We were not a sporting family, although my mother was captain of the tennis team while at UCD and Gránia was a popular sports captain in her school. So yes, there were sports *in* the family. Nothing physical for me, though. Sedentary games like chess, crosswords, puzzles, and fishing, although fishing can be physical insofar as landing a decent-sized salmon can be a strenuous battle. Walking along a riverbank can be slow and peaceful and quiet exercise.

Watching Des all my life, I don't think I ever saw him winded from physical activity. Me? Perhaps chasing a 48A bus so as not to be late for school. One shot at basketball in Loreto College on St Stephen's Green followed by a (fake) display of physical problems had made sure I was allowed off sports for ever, although a new nun in charge of sports had sent me out for – God forbid! – a hockey match. Well, that was easy ... easy, as by my third bully – one bully, two bully, three – I rolled on the ground pretending I'd broken my ankle.

On the basketball court I just kept forgetting the rules, getting on everyone's nerves until I was never picked for a team and sent indoors – in disgrace in their eyes, but a relief in mine. I got back into netball briefly, because the netball court was overlooked by the Catholic University School for boys and they threw us lollipops.

Watching sports does interest me, though – team sports, though I've never been on a team for longer than a day. Some individual sports like snooker engage me completely, to the point of watching the first ball potted to the last ball in the championships at Sheffield. Indeed, I made a break of sixty-nine on the BBC when I was doing a *Play for Today*.

So why do I question being lazy?

Catholicism despises laziness to the point of making it one of its seven deadly sins. In our house, there was an eighth; *never, ever owe money*. I'm eighty years old, and I never have, never do, and never will owe anyone a penny.

That's all terrifying when you're young. So terrifying that for the second time I took the thin rope from under the stairs, took all my clothes off, stood in front of the only full-length mirror in the house, on the inside of the wardrobe, and slowly, carefully, hooked it in a simple knot that Des had taught me using a fishing-line. Slowly, painfully I twisted it around my waist. I tightened and tightened it, heaving heavily as it hurt more and more. I tugged and strained and huffed and puffed, feeling holier and holier as I saw specks of blood coming through my child's fair skin. I tugged and tugged, tears falling down my face, causing me to feel like a true martyr for God, certain now of easy entry into heaven. This private torture almost achieved the 'ecstasy' described in the Bible and represented on the saints' cards, those images of painful martyrdom that my mother always brought home from the church.

Why Do I Cry?

No one reason I can think of. I've had no fights with anyone recently. No bad news. The opposite, in fact. I had the *best* news I've had in two years. I'm actually out of hospital. Free after twenty-four months in the Meath Hospital, being confined and being in pain. Now I'm free to go where I like with whoever I like. Do whatever I like. I should be smiling, but still my heart is dark.

All my life I've been like this. Moods changing. I go from giddiness to pain with no warning.

I have always felt a freak. And now my body is battered with bad luck. My brain perhaps battered before it properly formed. Whatever this darkness is, it lives happily in every pore of me, leaving me for months without light.

I have never cried so loud so quietly. Why do I cry now? Was it some new exhaustion? My limbs heavy as my heart?

'You've been through hell,' I told myself. 'Of course the body bends in preparation to stand tall again. This too shall pass.'

But it didn't. This time the tears were ominous.

I remember perfectly the very moment this nugget of clarity came to me. I was going up the stairs to bed, to rest. I was exhausted. Each step was slow and cumbersome. Near the top, I leaned over the banister and said to my mother, 'There's something wrong with me.'

I knew something was wrong, but everyone kept telling me to remember what I had been through in the last two years. That it was perfectly natural that I should feel tired. How my body would take a long time to readjust after the accident and the surgeries. As if I didn't know all that. *Jesus Christ, stop treating me like a five-year-old!* I knew my fucking body better than any of them did.

'What's wrong?' she asked.

Hearing fear in her voice, I felt a sudden burst of love for her. What had the last two years done to her? Her hair was grey now, her eyes were sad. Her anger at me was almost gone.

Suddenly terrified that I might break her heart again, and feeling a new adult compassion, I said, 'There's something not right with me. I feel too tired. Just call Dr Jackson. He'll have a magic potion, won't he?'

'Do you feel sick?' she asked, her voice weak as a child's.

'No. Not sick. But something's wrong.'

As I write these words, I can smell the breath of fear pouring from her as she said, 'Go to bed. Lie down. Rest. You've a lot to recover from. I'll phone Terry now.'

All I wanted was to be in my old bed again, so I turned back towards the stairs, leaving the rest of the family to cackle around in the kitchen, being helpful to my mother. I grabbed the rail and climbed up to the top step, where Gránia and I used to sit in our pyjamas, huddled together, stifling our giggles as we eavesdropped on our parents' conversations. I got to the top and fell over like a rag doll. Taken by surprise, I pulled myself into a sitting position, terrified someone would come out of the kitchen and see me like this. I had to get back into the bedroom. I tried again to stand but my knees buckled. Why? What in the name of God was wrong now? Had I done too much running around the hospital saying my goodbyes? *I know my legs are still weak,* I thought, *but not like this.*

I crawled across the landing to the bedroom door and pushed it open with my back. I climbed into my big old double bed. There I lay, gasping for breath. As my strength slowly returned, an avalanche of memories came from the walls of the room, drowning me in sadness, shutting down my weak body as I fell into a deep, deep sleep.

I must have slept for a long time, as now the sky was dark and there was a small tray on the chair beside my bed. A big glass of milk and two enormous slices of white bread with red jam piled so high that it had dribbled down onto the bedsheets.

Terry was the family doctor. A great friend of my father's. Another fisherman. A member of that very private Dublin club. He was an amazing doctor, head and shoulders above the rest with his God-given talent as a diagnostician. I knew that he'd find out what was wrong.

My mother's hand was gently tapping my shoulder. I felt so moved by her that it took me a minute to see a well-turned-out handsome young man standing at the end of my bed with a doctor's bag in his hand. There's something about those old-fashioned doctors' bags that engulfs me with hope and happiness. Apart from the classic design, their elegance and grace are so visually pleasing they always made me smile. So smile I did.

'Brenda,' Bina said, 'Dr Jackson is on holiday and this is Dr O'Leary, who's standing in for him.'

'Hello,' I said, struggling my body up into a sitting position. 'Hello.'

He gave the tiniest glance to Bina, making it clear he wanted her to leave the room.

This was a very important moment in my life.

Through all the long months and years I had spent in the company of doctors – in hospitals, in A & E departments, in sad waiting rooms, in posh, shiny waiting rooms – I had never had a one-on-one conversation with any of the doctors. An adult was always present. Usually Bina. Sometimes Des. Sometimes both. I got used to sitting across a desk, invisible to everyone, as they discussed my body.

But here I was, safe in my own bed, face to face with a young doctor who had shown me a new respect, treated me as capable of explaining my ailment clearly to him.

'Thank you for that,' I said emotionally, knowing he knew exactly what I meant.

He opened his beautiful bag, took out his stethoscope, and proceeded to do all the usual tests.

'You have no temperature, your blood pressure seems fine, and you say you have no pain,' he said, almost to himself.

'No. No pain. Just tired,' I said.

'Mmm. I think you've picked up some strain of a flu. There's one going around. Yes. That's more than likely what it is. So worry not, young lady. I'm going to give you a prescription for a tonic, which, if you take it three times a day, will have you running around within a week.'

He shook my hand and left the room.

Good news, then.

But something deep inside told me that this was not the case.

I slid back down under the heavy blankets and cried myself back into the darkness of sleep.

Terry had been away fishing but when he heard I wasn't well he came straight over to the house. I remember him standing at the foot of the bed, a handsome man with a moustache and a trilby hat. He didn't even have to examine me. He just smiled on me and said, 'Consumption hath no mercy on blue eyes and golden hair.'

I knew immediately what it meant.

Later that day, I heard my mother screaming downstairs. I had never heard a sound like it. It was terrifying. So lost, so full of fear. Slowly, I began to understand the words that she was shouting.

'We can't tell anyone!' she screamed. 'I'll keep her here at home. You can throw your desk out, Des, and I'll get a new bed for her and Terry can come and treat her. We *cannot* tell anyone, Des. Just think of the shame, the shame that will be brought upon us. We can say she has some other disease – something really contagious – to keep her friends away. Please, *please*, Des. Don't do this! Don't bring shame upon us all!'

They were shouting about me.

I froze. So, I was going to die, and she wanted me to die at home, not in hospital.

Now that I knew I was going to die, the fact that all I got from her was her selfish worry about the shame I would bring down on her made me feel utterly betrayed, and at the same time not surprised. I put my head into my hands and cried in fear and disappointment at this betrayal by my parents when I so desperately needed them.

Bina's mad wailing was suddenly broken by my father's voice raised in passionate anger as he shouted at her.

'Stop! For God's sake, Bina, will you pull yourself together? There is going to be no discussion about Brenda. Brenda is going out to the sanatorium in Blanchardstown *tomorrow*. You heard what Terry said. There'll be a bed ready for her.'

This was one of the three times in my life I had heard Des raise his voice. It shut Bina up completely. It shut me up too.

I heard him coming up the stairs. I went out to meet him, begging God to save me from his anger.

But as he got nearer, I watched him kneel on the step below me. I saw him stretch his arms out to hold my head in a way he had never done before, to bring me a kind of peace. To take away all that had ever happened to me and all that was now going to happen to me.

A teenaged Brenda.

He whispered quietly, 'Consumption hath no mercy on blue eyes and golden hair.'

'Kay Geddess?' I asked

'Yes, Brenda,' he said.

He brought me back to my bed, and he pulled the heavy blankets across my body as if it were made of glass. He kissed my forehead. He looked like a broken man.

'Everything will be all right,' he whispered. 'Your mother will see sense. You look so tired it breaks my heart and I have no magic wand,' he said as he stood up slowly, looking deep into my eyes. I saw how his own eyes were haunted and I knew that he would never look the same again.

He whispered gently, 'But not everyone dies from it.'

I was confined to a sanatorium in Blanchardstown for a

year. I saw nobody but the nurses for the first twelve weeks. Even after that, visiting was strictly limited. Friday evenings, one hour, for husbands and wives. Sunday afternoon, one hour for family and friends. Des couldn't come on Sundays because he had a radio show on RTÉ, *Down the Country with Fred Desmond*, but he got permission to come on a Friday night. So I had what every teenage girl must want: my father's attention, all to myself, for one hour each week, every week for ten months.

When I got a little better he bought me a small typewriter and said, 'Your letters are so lovely. You should do a little writing.'

Rehearsal – Arkle

Spending four weeks rehearsing a play for the theatre is better than sex. The theatre is where I fell passionately in love with acting, which probably began way back at the Father Mathew *feis*, when we were winning medals for acting.

Doing it professionally opened up my life into an enchanted world full of fascinating people. Within minutes of entering I knew this was my place: the smell, the sounds, the silence, the shapes, the shadows. The very *air* in those studios swept me off my feet. Several members of that group, those amazing people, became lifelong friends. People like Una Collins, Ginette Waddell, Iris Lawlor, Aiden Grennell, and Maureen Toal. Between them all they gave me confidence and gently led me down the path to where I now stand. Some of them even lived long enough to see me win The Prize.

Ginette was wonderful. She was what used to be called a 'spinster' and she lived in a flat on the top floor of 69 Merrion Square with high bay windows and a little semi-circular stair to an attic room where her father – Rutherford Mayne, a well-known playwright – lived. She was only the second person I had ever met who lived in a flat. We all lived in semi-detached, suburban Mr Jones houses.

Una taught me about make-up and nylon stockings. She bought me ribbons and braids and plaited my beautiful long blonde hair. Ginette washed and dried and combed and brushed my hair. She'd brush slowly, entertaining Rutherford, who'd sit on the big window ledge, watching and admiring me.

Ginette introduced me to so many things. One day I was with her on Henry Street when she darted into Arnott's and bought me a little box of assorted make-up. I felt like I had died and gone to heaven. I had to hide it from Bina, of course, but I loved it.

One day, not long after I came out of the sanatorium, she asked Bina and Des could she take me to the races. She said she planned to put a little money on a horse called Arkle and now we could go out together. She'd never heard of him but now she wanted to see him running in the flesh.

I'd no idea what to do when we got there. Ginette took me in and brought me straight up to the betting office and she placed a bet for herself and one for me. Then I just followed people around, doing what they did. I threw my body over the railings alongside the track, shouting and screaming and throwing my arms up in the air as everybody else was doing as Arkle crossed the line in first place.

I held the ticket tightly in my hand as we rushed up to collect the dosh. Everyone was hugging everyone as they moved to the winners' enclosure.

Ginette knew everyone. That's how we got in.

I remembered the sometimes dangerous beauty of a horse, which I knew about from Kerry. But this was not a Kerry horse. This was a champion. This was Arkle. I knew that we were privileged to be in the winners' enclosure, but it became serious for me when I was actually inside, looking out at the unchosen ones.

Although it was noisy, it was silent in a way that reminded me of that difference in the air Gránia and I had felt when we leaped over the communion rail during our raid on the church in Kerry. There was an awareness that you were walking on sacred ground.

He was an altar. *Arkle himself* was an altar. He was a brown horse with the odd bit of light in his mane, and eyes that were a little wild, once or twice showing their whites, bucking and jumping with the excitement. Everyone stood around staring at him, waiting for him to calm down.

I nearly fainted when the jockey Pat Taaffe turned around and beckoned me. I felt frozen to the ground, but he smiled and I took the ten steps or so to reach them. Mr Taaffe took my hand and placed it on Arkle's nose.

When my hand touched that extraordinary animal's nose, a bolt of all he was went right through me like an electric shock. He was on a high from the winning. His powerful body was shining with sweat. His horseshoes stamped on the ground as the steam rose from under the blanket across his back. The sheer majesty when he raised the whole front half of his body up into the air, dancing on his two back legs and neighing out a thundering laugh that made all the people laugh too. On all fours again, he moved towards me and gently laid his nose on my shoulder. He nuzzled his velvet mouth against my ear.

I could feel the envy sizzling all around me as Mr Taaffe handed me a lump of sugar.

'Give him that,' he said, putting it into the palm of my hand.

I held it out and this beautiful horse put out his long, pink tongue, then he suddenly shook his whole body from side to side, covering me in spit and sweat and guzzling up the sugar. It was like the wine and body of Christ.

People were gawking at me and drooling with envy as I reached up to put both my arms around his hot and sweaty neck. I kissed his warm pelt, thinking to myself, *If this is the thrill that addicts get from gambling on horses, then I'm in.*

First Grown-up Party (Rape)

I tried to escape childhood and find freedom in adulthood. But life landed lower blows than that and intimacies I had never dreamed of tied dragging ropes around my dreams of growing up.

At nearly eighteen, my health was much improved but, having missed out on so much of my education and on a normal teenage life, I was very immature. I was different. All through her life, Gránia would say I was never the same after the accident.

At my first grown-up party, I was standing awkwardly in the corner when a lovely young man came over, claiming that we had met before. I didn't remember him, but I got up and danced with him. After three or four songs, Elvis came on, singing 'Are you Lonesome Tonight?' To this thrilling sound, the young man led me down the hall and into the first bedroom on the right. I knew exactly what he wanted, but I was shy and a little nervous. I lay beside him on the bed. This was different from what I had known before.

Afterwards I lay back on the satin pillows and watched him re-dress the bits of his body he'd found necessary to undress in order to attack me. He said he would be leaving the party soon, and without even seeing my tears he asked could he give me a lift anywhere.

He tied his shoelaces and went to take my hand to bring me back to the party.

'Leave me alone,' I said.

Looking angry, he slammed the door behind him.

The trickle of warm blood I had felt on my thigh would be dry now, but I wanted to feel it. I went into the bathroom, stood on the side of the bath, and threw my leg up in the air to see it all more clearly.

Yes, there it was, or there it wasn't. He'd torn my knickers before pushing his fist straight up through my virgin hymen. Then he'd guided his long, hard penis roughly along the same path and, leaning on his elbows, he rode me for about five minutes, huffing and puffing and mumbling filthy words. Then he just stopped.

I sat there for what seemed like a long time. I dressed slowly, throwing the torn underwear into a bin before phoning Des. I went outside and sat my burning cunt down on the cool wall and waited.

To be deflowered with such casual cruelty would leave its mark on me for the rest of my life.

When we got home, I told Des what had happened. The blood drained from his face as he took me gently by the arm and led me back out to the car. I knew instinctively he was taking me to see Terry Jackson and I was right. Terry examined me and said that yes, I was no longer a virgin. He comforted me with lies, like that my hymen would repair itself. Des comforted me with the words he'd been saying since I told him what happened: not all men are like that, he said. Instinctively, the three of us agreed that my mother must never know the truth about this.

This incident, more than any other, changed me. I was broken now and would remain so.

Hair Sale

I was eighteen, and on an 'exchange' in Valencia. The son of the house, Carlos, had been sent to Bina in Dublin, who was treating him like a king, giving him the best of everything, but the Gómez family were certainly not treating me like a queen. I'd sat with them in their huge dining room for the first two days and then I'd been brought downstairs by a maid.

I stayed downstairs and had a ball with the maids, who became my family in Spain. I learned Spanish from them very quickly and they showed me all the beautiful architecture in Valencia; I enjoyed myself immensely, and was perfectly content.

But Gránia was furious. She was in living in Spain, staying in a room above the bookshop she was working in. But the shop folded and they were selling the building so she had to leave. Serendipity for me.

Gránia arrived, pulled my suitcase out and told me to pack my clothes. She took my arm and marched me up to the sitting room to talk to Señora Gómez and tell them I was leaving.

I was mortified. Gránia grabbed me by the arm, took the suitcase, and brought me downstairs, where we left it with the porter. We went across the road to a little café where she explained what was going on. She was really angry, talking about how well Bina was treating Carlos, and how awfully his family was treating me. She was livid. I was surprised and shocked at her level of anger. I admired her bravery. This impressively protective act left us without a roof over our heads and no transport, but also no fear, no regrets, and a great love.

'That'll show them!' I said loudly.

'Well,' she answered, 'how dare they do that to you? And the way Bina is treating their son back in Dublin!'

'Oh God!' I cried, realizing how disobedient this all was. 'Mammy! Dublin! Carlos! What'll happen now?'

'Never mind,' Gránia said. 'Let me think.'

It was around noon, mid-July, coming up to the worst heat of the day. We sat by the fountain in the square. Gránia had her thinking cap on; I could hear it working. I leaned back, catching the edge of the cool water on my head and letting it dribble all the way down my back into the crack of my bottom.

I was doing what I had been doing since I had set foot in Spain three months before. I was gazing at Spanish boys, beautiful Spanish boys, their elegance and arrogance always on display. It was their skin. In Ireland, before there were cheap flights, we had potato-coloured skin. Pasty. These boys were golden. They took my breath away. Not a pimple or a blackhead in sight, not a hint of acne. Each one looked as if he'd just been dipped in honey.

And their teeth! Wow! I didn't know one single person in Ireland who had good teeth. It was in Spain I realized the power of the smile, the power of a confident mouth. If you want to throw your head back and laugh out loud, it really should only be done with a mouthful of stunning choppers.

That's something I'll never do, as all my teeth were knocked out in the accident when I was fourteen. That was the beginning of my lifelong battle with false teeth. Back then, Irish dentistry was butchery. It was actually fashionable to have false teeth.

I basked in the beauty of these little gods. They smiled, they laughed, they dazzled the world with their flashlight smiles. They'd probably never been to a dentist in their lives. They would probably never have to go.

I was concentrating on a particularly gorgeous waiter weaving in and around the café tables on the street when Gránia poked my arm.

'How much money have you got?' she asked.

'Ouch,' I said, rubbing my arm as I checked my dress pockets. 'Not much,' I mumbled. 'We left so fast I left my purse behind. There must have been a hundred pesetas in there.'

'Never mind,' she said. 'C'mon, c'mon.'

Gránia held her arm out for me to link. I loved that. The Frickers weren't very physically affectionate – nobody Irish really was back then – but I was and I *am*. I love simple things, linking arms with someone I love. We took two lefts and stopped outside a hairdressing salon – a very smart one.

Oh! I thought, taking a quick breath. *She's taking me to a proper hairdresser to get my long golden hair washed. To cheer me up.*

But the place was shut already for the siesta. I had been surprised to discover that siesta time was exactly that: at two in the afternoon the shops shut and people went home and they went to bed, where they slept for about three hours. Then they got up and went back to work until around nine or ten, and then they had their main meal of the day. I was beginning to like this routine.

Gránia got irritated again. She read a phone number from one of the ads in the window, then rooted for a pencil in her ever-present overloaded linen bag, with which she wrote the number down.

'Are you going to get your hair washed?' I asked her.

Gránia, in her late teens.

Ignoring me, she changed the subject: 'Let's go over there for a couple of empty wine bottles.'

My ears pricked up and I grinned as I knew exactly what that meant: a trip to a *bodega*! Basically a wine shop, but with a service whereby you brought in an empty bottle and went into an eerily quiet room full of barrels lying neatly on their sides on individual low tables. Each barrel had a little silver tap with a small tray on the floor underneath to catch drips. There were labels on each barrel, with the name, region, and colour of the wine within. The floor was sandy, which kept the place cool and quiet. You brought your empty bottle in and picked a barrel. Then they filled it with your wine of choice, smoothly twisted a cork into the neck, accepted your ten or twenty pesetas, and smiled their beautiful smiles before saying *adios*.

Gránia and I walked up and down reading the labels, as if we had a clue as to what was written on any of them. I caved well before I wanted to, pointing to a barrel of red and saying, '*Este vino, por favor.*' The young gods silently took our empty bottles and laid them on the cool floor. Then they whipped a sparkling white cloth out from nowhere and leaned over to lay it across the little silver tap before picking up our empty bottles and preparing corks for them. I could not take my eyes off one of them. His legs went on for ever, with the best bits disappearing up into his short shorts. A generous little bulge, too.

Gránia and I sat together on a cold marble bench and watched the show.

The boys waited till we were still and then opened the window. A welcome early afternoon breeze blew gently in. They got their little stools – three-legged ones, just like the milking stools in Kerry – and pulled themselves towards the barrels of our choice with such confidence they made me laugh.

'Which one do you fancy?' I asked Gránia, nudging her in the ribs.

'*Stop it*, Brenda!' she responded with her Holy Mary voice.

'The most handsome one of the two?' I whispered. 'The one on the left or the one on the right?'

'Okay then,' she whispered, 'there's not a whiff of a differ-ence between them but, now that you're asking, I like *el chico de la derecha.*'

I agreed with her but, for the sake of divilment, said, 'He wouldn't be interested in you. You have the one on the left, and I'll take the one on the right.'

With that, he kicked the sand away, pushed back his stool, stood full height, slipped a label from the counter, licked it with his perfect pink tongue, and smoothed it around the curve of the dark red bottle. He wrote a word on the label, balanced the bottle on his forearm, and then rolled it down into my waiting palms. My boy was quicker than Gránia's, giving me a chance to watch her grunt with the weight, or perhaps with pleasure of nearly missing the bottle but catching it.

Gránia was worrying about cash now. She counted out the notes and coins, and turned away slightly to cover up the fact that we were short of money, but these boys understood. They both smiled from ear to ear, saying that as we were the first people they'd ever met from Ireland, the wine would be a gift.

We walked out of the *bodega* into the boiling heat. I almost fainted, but Gránia was used to it because she'd been in Spain for six months already. We walked slowly in the murderous sunshine. The excitement of getting out of captivity was cooling me off, what with beautiful boys and the glorious city. I felt quite giddy as we giggled our way back to the main square, each with a bottle of wine under her arm, grown-up and seriously European. We sat back exactly where we'd been an hour earlier, and Gránia leaned over to another Adonis sitting beside us and asked him to take the cork out of one of our bottles. He put his newspaper down and, lifting the bottle to his mouth as if to drink, he clamped his perfect white teeth around the cork and in one swift move, he pulled it out. He waved the open neck under his nose, and then took a swig of the wine. '*Bueno! Muy bueno!*' he said, as he handed bottle and cork back to Gránia, blinding us with his magnificent teeth.

'Okay,' Gránia said, changing her mind and putting the cork back in. 'I've got a plan. We're going to take the tram to the beach. We'll drink some wine there and decide what to do next.'

'But where in the name of God are we going to sleep tonight?' I asked.

She ignored me as we jumped on the tram and rattled and rolled our way out to the beach. There, it was quiet and lovely. We strolled along, each of us carrying our full bottle of wine.

When we passed guys on the beach, they just pointed at our wine, smiled shiny white-teeth smiles, and said, '*Fiesta? Sí? Sí?*'

'*Sí, sí sí!*' we answered freely, laughing into their handsome faces.

We were getting tired now. We had been in the heat for several hours and the sun was still strong. Gránia pointed at two big old trees with long, bending branches that curved out, creating a lovely shade for us to lie down in. We walked over and flopped into the shadow. As our bums hit the hot sand, we started to laugh, almost hysterically. We had, after all, had a very eventful day. It was terrifying, insofar as I had no idea what the hell we would do next.

I felt at one with Gránia. After all, we were having this adventure together because I had told her the truth about how I was being treated by the Spanish family, relegated downstairs and kept out of sight. *She* was the one who had jumped into action, defending me again, as she had so often. Gránia's defence of me was so frequent, I hardly saw it, and seldom – if ever – did I tell her how safe she made me feel.

We had buried the two red bottles in the sand to keep them out of the sun. We'd seen the locals do that. We dug one up, dusted it down, and struggled for ten minutes to get the cork out. Weak wrists run in our family. Then, with a wild *yippee*, we took turns to sip. No gulping! We had learned that much in Spain.

The silly babbling that comes with the first two mouthfuls of wine passed quicker than usual. We were only halfway down the bottle when we both fell fast asleep, our *vino tinto* lulling us to siesta. How lucky we were to have chosen the shade of that tree, because we slept the deep sleep of two slightly pissed young Irish girls. Looking back, I am astonished that neither of us feared being mugged, or raped, or worse. We were as safe as if we'd slept out in our back garden at home in Dublin.

When we woke in the morning, the beach had quite a few people on it, taking their daily swim in the cooler morning sun. There were lots of little Spanish kids, all of whom you wanted to sweep into your arms and run away with. Feeling hot and sticky after my sleep, I said that I, too, was going for a swim. Gránia would come as well, she said. She had her bikini with her, in her bag.

'Where's your bikini?' Gránia asked.

'It's in the fucking suitcase!' I answered, cranky in the morning as I always was.

'You mean you've no bikini?'

'I've just *said* that.'

'Well, then you can't go for a swim!'

'I *can* go for a swim,' I retorted. 'Watch this!'

I tore off my dress, revealing clean panties and a clean bra, which looked very much like a bikini to me.

'Goodbye!' I said, running towards the sea.

I was actually very self-conscious of my body, which was still as white as snow, but I kept going and made it to the shoreline and stepped carefully into the Mediterranean Sea. I could hear Gránia running behind me. She plunged under the water, emerging mid-flow, with the coolest, most rhythmic overarm stroke I'd ever seen. I stood with the water up to my knees and watched her flip smoothly onto her back.

'C'mon in,' she said sarcastically. 'We'll do another lesson,' she taunted, knowing I was a bad swimmer.

'Ah, shut up,' I answered. 'Leave me alone. You know I'm not a good swimmer. I'm going back to lie down.'

There was loads of space under the overhanging branches we had discovered the day before. The morning passed beautifully. I spent it drifting into the sea, and then getting out to lie in the sun, carefully keeping an eye out for midday, as I had learned the hard way by having the back of my neck painfully sunburned on my first two or three trips to the beach.

Suddenly I was hungry. I shouted to Gránia, 'I'm hungry!' I knew that would get her out of the water.

'Okay,' Gránia said. 'Go up and bury the second bottle of wine again. We can get something to eat and come back to it when we want it.'

'Good thinking, boss.'

I dug into the sand like a dog and buried the second bottle of wine. We got on the tram and once again I was amazed by how much noise twenty Spaniards could make, all talking at once.

We hopped off at the tram stop and bought some bread and cheese, which satisfied our hunger. Then we linked arms, walked back across the road and went past the little *bodega* and around the corner back to the hairdresser's we'd been to before. It was four o'clock now, and the salon was open – and blissfully air-conditioned.

It was very grand indeed. Tall antique mirrors hung along each wall. There was subtle lighting that was instantly relaxing. Inside were four big chairs, much like the ones I had seen in barber shops but covered with a dark red velvet cloth. It was almost decadent. Each chair faced its own complex set of mirrors. No matter which way you turned in it, you could see your head from different angles.

The sound of a slow violin played through the room as I took my place on a dark green velvet sofa, watching Gránia in serious conversation with what looked like the boss lady. Both their heads were turned, looking at me, as they chatted like thieves. Then the two of them came over, explaining to me that the hairdresser had a policy of giving free hair treatments if the customer was willing to have the whole procedure done by a student.

By God, Gránia is a genius! I thought. She'd done it again, organizing something for nothing that would make me feel pampered and groomed.

I had beautiful golden hair, way down past my waist. Looking after it in Ireland, in the rain and wind, was an awful chore but here all I had to do after a swim was walk on the beach for ten minutes and it was bone dry. I had never cared for my hair at home, but here in Spain, in the glorious sunshine, in a place where having blonde hair was very unusual, I saw for the first time that it was beautiful. I had become quite suave about receiving compliments on my hair.

Gránia was always very nice to me about my hair. Hers, although gloriously soft, was mousy, the same colour as that of thousands of other girls. Looking back, I think that I was probably a bit of a show-off about my hair. So what, though? I liked very little else about myself.

A very austere, handsome lady in her middle years flapped a cotton cape high into the air like a bullfighter with his red cloak, landing it perfectly around my neck. She clicked the hook and eye into place and then started to pump the chair with her strong leg. It felt wonderful being pumped up like that.

Next, the lady Gránia had been talking to came over and introduced herself as Consolata. She proceeded to turn on the charm to the point of hypnotizing me.

Little did I know that this was part of a plan.

Consolata stood behind me and with man-strong hands began to run her fingers through my hair.

'Qué bueno,' Consolata murmured. 'Qué bueno, qué bueno. Sí, sí, sí. Hermosa.'

I purred like a kitten, delighted with myself about the whole situation.

Suddenly, Consolata pulled at my beautiful long, golden-blonde locks. She yanked it into the air, draping it around the back of the chair like a golden cape. Her eyes lit up with pleasure as she spread it out behind me.

Suddenly, the most stunning silver blade I had ever seen caught my eye. It was shining in the sunlight, nestling among the other hair-cutting tools. It was a very sharp blade, reflecting daylight from the ceiling-to-floor windows. I was riveted by it, heady from the ambience of the room, and almost dizzy from the past twenty-four hours. I planned to steal it at the first opportunity.

But then, with a speed and strength that I can still physically feel today, Consolata scooped every rib of my hair into her hands, pulled it up into a ponytail, and then pulled it firmly towards her body. Holding the hair up like a sheet, she took a step back and shouted out, '*Ahora, ahora, ahora!*' It was like the starter gun at a racetrack.

As I reeled, startled by how loud her voice was, from the corner of my eye I saw a very large Spanish man appear from nowhere, brandishing what looked like gardening shears. He moved like lightning, as did the three or four other helpers who had arrived from nowhere. They were all holding my hair out now, and with one fantastic sweep, this man cut off all my long, golden-blonde locks, which fell into the waiting silken sheet held by the helpers.

For the first and last time in my life so far, I fainted. In fact, the shock was so profound, I think I fainted several times over. I cried and screamed, 'You're a traitor, Gránia!' but she was standing and laughing. Indeed, the large man and all the women and all the other people in the salon were laughing at me. I felt I had been beheaded.

As I cried and wailed, they got me back onto the chair and set about styling the stumps that had been left sticking out of my head. They ended up giving me a very smart, tailored, boyish hairstyle that I would keep for years. But at that moment I was livid with my sister.

When the whole ritual was over, Gránia leaned in and kissed my cheek.

'Well done, Brenda,' she said. 'Very well done. Now you can relax. Let's go.'

I got off the chair and followed Gránia into a shabby, ugly, dark back room, where Consolata sat behind a big oak desk. The contrast with the salon was quite shocking, but I watched as Consolata took a black tin from under the desk, placed it in front of her, and opened the box, where there was the biggest bunch of paper money I had ever seen. Something in me stirred. *What was this?* I asked myself.

Gránia ordered me to sit down. She was still grinning like a Cheshire cat. I wanted to hit her. I watched, bug-eyed, as the pile of cash that Consolata was counting out got bigger and bigger and bigger. She wrapped the notes in a piece of silk and handed it to Gránia, inviting her to check the amount. But trusting her, Gránia just took the white silk knapsack full of cash, turned her flushed face to me, and winked. When Consolata gave her what looked suspiciously like a receipt, the penny dropped.

I was about to scream at Gránia but she just grabbed my arm and whisked me out the door. We sat up on a big window-sill outside. She held the white silk package of cash up in the air, grinning from ear to ear.

'Did you just sell my hair?' I gasped.

'I did!' she said.

'Good God,' I replied. 'Was that money for my hair?'

'Yes,' she said, and pulled a silly face at me.

'There's *thousands* of pesetas in there!' I cried.

'Yes, Brenda.' She smiled. 'Thousands and thousands!'

We fell off the deep end, into hysterical, mad laughter, bending back and forth, slapping each other on the shoulder and screeching out again and again: 'We sold the hair! We sold the hair!' Soon we were jumping up and down, exhibiting uncontrollable delight so unruly that we caused a little public stir. But we weren't in Ireland, so passers-by could see that we were delirious with happiness for some good reason; back home they would have called an ambulance for us.

'*Olé, olé olé!*' they cried out to us, handsome boys and women alike. '*Chicas bonitas!*'

Suddenly I realized that Gránia had been planning this for days. She must have known that that hairdresser bought hair. What she did not know was that natural, long, golden-blonde North European hair was worth a fortune: more than any other kind or colour. Wig-makers would sell their souls for it.

My hair was gold dust to them. And now it was gold dust for us too.

Bullfight

I think I enjoyed the first bullfight I saw, and Gránia was hor-rified that I did. So I said we should go again and give it another go. And the second time we went, I was horrified too. I was horrified by the cruelty, the baying crowds, the panting, and the extended agonies of the bull. I had admired the gor-geousness and arrogance of the bullfighters. How they carried their young bodies in such an elegant, unnatural, manner. Their sparkling costumes, their sideways black hats, their white socks and their hornpipe shoes. The sexy way they swayed and bent and danced and stamped their feet while waving their silver swords in the sun and swirling their red cloaks, taunting those poor bulls with mesmerizing style.

But the second time it felt different than before. It was unbearable. And at the end, when the bull was about to be killed, we grabbed the little plastic cushions we were sitting on and flung them into the ring in a hopeless demonstration of our horror. Suddenly, there were four white-gloved hands on our shoulders. We knew at once that this was the dreaded *Guardia Civil*. They were the most feared section of the police force, and before we could say 'boo' we were dragged forcibly from our seats and thrown outside the bullring.

The Little Café

Gránia got me a job in a little café after she rescued me from that family. It was one of the best jobs I ever had. A few tables outside and a few tables inside. There were also a few bedrooms for rent, like an Irish B&B. Here they called them *pensiones*.

There were three or four stunningly sexy waitresses who dressed to kill and had social skills to die for and were so lovely to me, helping me along with my broken Spanish. I vividly remember their kindness and the atmosphere of fun and warmth.

I worked from eight to six. It was mainly a night café, so I would often stay on and sit at one of the little tables outside. Not only for the atmosphere, but also to watch the men, young and old, who frequented the place. There were a few regular guys who came on a Monday and a Friday and I became very close to them. I felt safe and protected by them.

One day, Gránia arrived with a face as white as a sheet. She put down her shopping, grabbed a cigarette, and pulled on it as if her life depended on it. (Which it did. It took that life early, when she was aged sixty-eight. Clogged lungs.)

'What's wrong?' I asked.

There was a long pause before she answered. She whispered

something. It was something we'd both inherited from Des, who spoke almost inaudibly when there was bad news.

'Brenda, we have to pack up. Now.'

'Now?'

'Now ...'

'Why?'

'... and head for Paris.'

'*Paris?*' I asked, excited at the thought of going to that romantic city.

'Here,' she said, handing me a bundle of pesetas. 'You pay the *pensión* while I pack.'

She moved swiftly and disappeared up the stairs before I was off my seat. In the blink of an eye we were filling the car with petrol and driving fast towards the French border.

It was on that extraordinary drive from Valencia to Paris that Gránia explained to me that the sweet little café I had been working in was in fact a sweet little brothel run by a relative of one the people who owned the bookshop. We must have driven for ten or fifteen minutes before I could speak, I was so utterly confused. A brothel? A *brothel*! So all those beautiful girls were prostitutes? And all those lovely men were johns? I could hear Gránia's low, quiet laugh as she leaned over and stroked my hair, offering comfort and reassurance.

It was at times like this that my mind would open. She was probably the only person who recognized my raw hunger to learn. She recognized the tragedy of a bright kid losing all her early schooling to illness. She recognized that I was struggling with reality. That I was dangerously innocent. She was violently protective of me, which gave me the freedom to run riot in the trust and the knowledge she gifted me.

She gave me the freedom to learn.

Working at the *Irish Times*

I was sitting in my *Irish Times* office with my boss Ken Gray, the arts editor. As usual, I was doing fuck all. Nepotism at its best. Thank you, Daddy.

The office was on the same floor as the photographers, of whom there were six. They had one big room for all their gear, and one big dark room where they developed their films. They were a lovely, rowdy bunch of boys. I remember Gordon and Jack, who as they brought me into the dark room to show me how films were developed, would also pinch my bum and kiss my cheek in a lovely, playful way that today would be regarded as sexual assault.

Every morning, a little man called Donal O'Donovan would come into the office. He would leave a small piece of paper, inscribed with numbers 1-3, 11-5, 4-2, on my desk, smile at me, and walk away.

I had no idea what it meant. I just left it there.

Then I was in the Pearl Bar, just two steps away from the *Irish Times* – where we all drank when we were supposed to be working – and so was Donal. It was a pub full of exciting people. I even met Myles na gCopaleen, Flann O'Brien, in there one day, with his small, black hat and his pale face. I bought him a drink. Oh, the drink made me brave.

I was at the bar with Donal. We were chatting about this and that.

'I give up,' I said, 'what are the numbers all about?'

He took out the paper and turned it over.

'Do you read the leading article?' he asked.

'I do.'

'Well, figure it out.'

I turned to look at the leading article again. It was about Cyprus. The Greek and Turkish Cypriots were fighting. Okay.

'The clue is on the page,' he said with a wink.

I couldn't break the code, so he began to explain it to me. The first number was the line. The second number was the word in that line. For example, 1-2 was 'The'. 11-5 was 'Greek' and '4-2' was 'Café', which meant, 'I'll meet you at the Greek Café.' He was asking me out.

We went out together for years, and we became great friends. He took me out for long drives. He had the same kind of car as Mary Lavin, a convertible Morris Minor. He explained so much to me about books, about news, about articles that Des should have done when he worked there but never did. He was lovely. He reminded me of Séamus S.

*

My father was working at the department of agriculture as the public relations officer to Charlie Haughey, who was the minister. He loved it and always said that Charlie Haughey was the best boss he ever had. He knew what he wanted, asked you to do it, and appreciated it when you did. It was as simple as that, according to Des.

Sometimes they'd have to meet to catch up on the day's business. This wasn't always done in Merrion Street. Charlie liked the elegant, up-market hotel called The Russell.

Because Des used to give me his car when he was working, there were one or two occasions when I had to collect him at the hotel, which meant going in and sitting with them until they were finished business. Charlie Haughey was a plain man with a fish-like face, but my goodness me, he was sexy. He flirted outrageously with me, much to the discomfort of my father.

They were heady days. I mixed with bright, intelligent people who always included me in their conversations. One of the best things I got from working in the *Irish Times* was my lifelong friendship with Donal.

Feeling Safe While Working
(Acting)

When I was working, I felt safe.

In those days, everyone involved in the theatre in Dublin drank in Neary's, the Flowing Tide, or Davy Byrne's. In this strange way, the pubs were crucibles of talent. The love of language that had first been nurtured in me by Ena Burke now drew me to like-minded people.

In Dublin of the 1960s, theatre was a thriving art form, and people were drawn to it not from the desire to be famous but because of a love of storytelling and the art of performance. Various theatre stalwarts, including Phyllis Ryan, who had a small production company, and the director Jim Fitzgerald, took an interest in me, and gave me work.

One day I was drinking in Neary's yet again. It was a great pub where we all talked and laughed and got drunk together. It was full of actors, musicians, and writers. On this day, I was slightly pissed when Jim Fitzgerald came running in, shouting as usual.

'Fricker, Fricker, Fricker, where are you? They are rehearsing a play on Molesworth Hall in Molesworth Street,' he said. 'They're doing a production of Brecht's *Mother*

Courage with Siobhán McKenna playing the lead. The costumes are being designed by Micheál Mac Liammóir, and Hilton Edwards is director. It needs lots and lots of extras. So get yourself down there. You never know; you might get a job.'

I ran down. They gave me a job, paying five quid a week. My first professional acting job.

Micheál Mac Liammóir, who I had seen do *The Importance of Being Oscar*, a one-man show about Oscar Wilde, was absolutely brilliant. The ticket consisted of a booklet containing the complete script of the show. I must have read it a hundred times, and loving every word that Oscar Wilde wrote, it wasn't long before I knew the whole thing by heart from beginning to end. I went to see the show thirteen times. The last time I went, I had a cheap seat in one of the boxes, where you had to lean across to even see the stage. He was in full flow and I knew that at this stage of his life, he was going blind. The set was simple. A couple of chairs and a little table with a jug of water and a glass. He walked around so gracefully, linking poetry and play together, quoting chunks from *De Profundis*, which made me weep. The last time I saw it, he was walking around and suddenly he dried. He was lost. He couldn't remember the next line. Nobody in the theatre knew this except me. Because I knew it off by heart, I leaned over and almost prompted him. I slapped my hand on my mouth to stop myself and listened in amazement as he ad-libbed his way out of the problem, continuing the flow with his deep knowledge of Oscar Wilde to bring him smoothly back to where he'd lost the thread. I was gobsmacked. I wanted to clap loudly and jump up and down and shout hoorah but obviously I couldn't. I'd noticed over the thirteen times that I saw the show that he was getting visibly older.

By the time I joined the cast of *Mother Courage*, he had slowed down considerably. I couldn't believe that I was being introduced to him. That he actually shook my hand, smiled at me, and said in that velvety, musical voice, 'You're very welcome, Brenda, but we have a problem. I've run out of black shawls.'

The women extras in *Mother Courage* are peasants, and they need shawls.

'I can get you some!' I said.

'My darling girl! If you can help in any way, that would be much appreciated.'

I don't think he believed me. I ran home, ran up to Bina, and said: 'Phone Nonee!'

There was one phone in Gneeveguilla, in the post office, and they'd go down and get you if there was a call.

'For what?' she asked.

'For shawls,' I said.

When I explained, she phoned. Someone fetched Nonee, who came and phoned us back.

'Brenda wants you to do something for her,' Bina said. 'Here she is.'

'Nonee, Nonee,' I cried. 'I need black shawls. Go round the village and get every black shawl that you can and post them up to me.'

A big cardboard box arrived days later. I put it in the boot of the car, drove straight to Molesworth Street and shouted out: 'Tell Micheál I've got loads of shawls for him!'

There was great excitement as he came slowly down the stairs, with people all around him smiling and whispering, 'We've got the shawls! We've got the shawls!'

The box was unloaded from the boot and carried into the rehearsal room where it was opened up. All the shawls were pulled out and waved in the air, waiting for Micheál to come in.

When he did, I grabbed a shawl, ran up, and threw it around his shoulders. He roared with laughter and delight. He kissed me on both cheeks saying, 'My darling, darling girl! Where in heaven did you get these?'

We became firm friends. I went to see him when he was dying in hospital, a frail old man. I sat down and held his hand and whispered my name.

'The shawls, the shawls,' he whispered back.

I stayed for a while and then I went up to Neary's and got drunk. A few days later, I received a handwritten letter, thanking me for going in to see him, and thanking me again for the shawls, the shawls, the shawls.

He died a week later.

There was a lovely man called Robert Carrickford, the union representative for Equity, the actors' union. He'd follow me around with bits of paper saying: 'You have to sign this, Brenda!' Everywhere I went he was there: 'You have to sign this!'

Eventually I did and became a signed-up member of Equity. I'd been working without being a member of the union until then. I listen to the kids today talking about striving to become a member of the union. The difference is quite shocking. The ease with which these things happened all those years ago.

Tolka Row

I was sitting in Neary's pub with Donal McCann having a quiet lunchtime pint when suddenly the door burst open and in ran Jim Fitzgerald again. Jim was an excellent man. He was small with a slightly twisted spine, an eagle eye, and an intellect to equal any in the country. He was a man of courage, staging Beckett, Friel, and Shakespeare in modern and exciting ways. And now he was directing the first episode of Ireland's first ever soap opera for television, *Tolka Row*. He slid in along the bench, feigning collapse and gasping for a pint.

'Brenda Fricker! I've found you! Brenda Fricker! Brenda! Fricker, Fricker, Fricker, Fricker. I LOVE that name! But, seriously, we're writing in a part to play Jimmy Bartley's girlfriend. A hotel receptionist. It should be about ten episodes. Are you interested?' He laughed, knowing that I was unemployed, that I'd never done television, and was keen as mustard to work with him.

Laughing at his antics, I hugged him, saying, 'Of course, of course!' I linked his arm, kissed his cheek, ordered another round of drinks, and settled back to hear his story. Eventually the pints arrived, interrupting the chatter. But, as it turned out, it wasn't just chatter. He was serious. RTÉ was about to actually film a soap opera! I'd heard something vaguely and remembered that Jimmy Bartley – an actor friend of mine – had something to do with it. Other than that, I knew nothing about it. But I liked the idea of work. Of working with Jim. The idea of a job. A job on television! I sipped my pint, puffed on my cigarette, and said, 'Why not?'

'Hooooorah!' Jim shouted, jumping up and crawling along the bench-top across Donal's shoulders like a cat. He plonked himself beside me, grabbed my face with both hands, and kissed me so hard on the mouth that I yelped. We brushed easily through a cuppla pints, fingering through the pages of the first episode, which he'd brought with him. Donal, who was normally very laid-back, got as excited as we were. Last orders were called before we realized how late it was. By now we were well pissed and happy. It seemed a lovely script and I was bursting with curiosity to see what it was like to work in television. I drove home after agreeing to be at rehearsals at ten the next morning. Bina was beside herself with excitement and Des just looked up from his book and said, 'That's wonderful, Brenda. Let's see how it goes.'

My character in this soap opera was called Joan Broderick. It was all set in a housing estate on Dublin's Northside, where the Tolka river flows. It was based on the play *Tolka Row*, written by Maura Laverty, and it was the station's first drama series, a saga about the Nolans and the Feeneys, two working-class Dublin families. Joan was the girlfriend of the character of handsome Jimmy Bartley, who had a much bigger part than me.

Tolka Row became primetime viewing, despite the fact that in those days there was no concept of soap operas as having any sort of cultural importance. I'd love to see some of those episodes again, but RTÉ wiped all the episodes after broadcast in order to use the videotapes again. Apparently just the final episode remains in the archives.

Mad

I woke up face down on a wet cold floor my face was drenched
in the sea or in the bath I couldn't move I think I screamed
I know I kicked out at the air there was a wall the place was
thick my clothes were gone

I stretched again and found I know not what naked now
and thrown away I heard a sound so far away a song rang
out and I can hear it now quite clearly every day a blank a
saviour in an empty head an end somewhere a face in mine
saying I was safe and that was true the walls were warm
again hot liquid now a needle in a vein a soft goodbye to
part of me I'd lost somewhere along the way I'd told myself
to take them all against the grain to help my brain my stifled
brain my broken brain I'm told the bits just rot inside of
you is that the pain? That must be it it must be that it claws
insanely from the inside out and brings its own insanity the
kitchen plates they threatened me they had to go they're full
of hate and so am I I'm drenched in it can you not taste the
smell I shouted out and flung them all against the wall as
light as feathers now they flew and shattered to the floor I
told myself that this was mine I slowly bent to suck the blood
off of my feet I watched the blood smile up at me I watched
it kiss my mouth and swallow me I rolled and kissed the edge
of every bit the shattered shameful bits not threatening now

a feast of blood again it rolled along my lips straight from my abandoned brain into my abandoned mouth the jagged edges stroked my skin to make it leak the floor was wet so that was it no sea no bath just rotten bits of me red lakes of me that brought me ecstasy that made me weak and wanting more of this salacious stuff within my head it tortured me it tried to make me live when all I saw was something else that screamed to me to try again

Two days later I woke up all bandaged up in thick white strips of gauze white stuff was everywhere my face was sore my heart was gone I heard the words Miss Smarty Pants you've failed again so that was it Sweet Nurse Divine as she was called she grabbed me by my hair again pulled back my head to stuff a bunch of tablets down my throat the shame the shame she spat into my face the shame disgrace she spat at me the shame disgrace she spat again her smelly spit was spurting out between her teeth her great big yellow teeth she dribbled bile on me she spoke she spat while shouting loudly on my face oh madam Fricker here again for that same sin that sickly sin that sin that sin you've failed again Miss Smarty Pants that's all you've done you've failed again

A cell a bed a light somewhere alone and lonely now a noise a face a prick into a vein a cloud again and then the joy of sleep again to dream again to hear that noise again of people telling me I'd failed again

The opposite to life is certainly not death the opposite to cold is certainly not heat the opposite to me is certainly not you but now I'm here within the walls outside the walls mad people walk I know because I heard them there I heard the screams those weak thin sickly screams that hide behind the shrillest shrieks of all the ones locked in the ones locked out and here I was my arms were bound again I can't reach out I can't reach in I'm gagged by drugs I'm nearly dead but bits of brain still scream at me is this the shape? Is this the end?

*I walked into the feeling I was feeling and I grabbed it tight
to keep it safe too often dreams were robbed from me robbed
before I got to know them well I had to keep those my feelings
safe and hope some god would help them out to find a place
to hide or find a place to kill them all to put my body into one
piece to make it breathe again in and out finding strength I
walked straight over to a door I opened it with just my eyes
nothing there but a wild wild wind which flung me round and
threw me onto that white chair the one I'd seen when coming
in the one I'd catched out of the corner of my eye I pinched
myself and saw myself sitting up in bed awake a million miles
from he who threatened with repeating dreams while calling
out to all of them to hurry back into the deal to stay with me
to come and see inside of me to see inside of me and you will
see the truth of men was I the inside of inside him would he no
longer walk with me would he no longer walk all over me. or
would I kiss the hanging flaps of skin again or was she fearful
now of all the lies she'd tell she twisted them so often now and
she was bored as one lie danced inside the other lie the other
lies that lived beneath her tongue the ones that ran to rescue
her from curiosity the ones that would punch out lights and
leaves wet leaves for her to lie on the best lies lived with me
the best lies loved with me always there to rescue me my life
was in my head it went inside on sunny days and when I knew
the sky was falling down on me I'd duck and dodge until the
rain washed out the blurry lines of me I'd find my silence there
while leaving all the lies outside beside my dreams all broken
into tiny pieces now like me they died an awful death and now
they're there they're lying there upon the dirty floor and after
all of this and after all of this there's nothing that has flipped
the switch to steer me down a road of sanity my brain just
broke again mad screams again my hands were pushing glass
again and pushing it into my mouth the sky was bright the
walls were dark my head was in between and caught tight in*

a vice of dying life I'm sorry now I told myself I'm sorry Ma
for kicking you I'm sorry Ma for doing you wrong I'm striving
now to show the pain the knowledge of the pain of it the shil-
lings and the pence of it I'm sorry too for ending it

    And then I heard me scream again aware of whispers now
somehow close now and then I turned and hissed again the
stupid fools I ran and ran with all the speed of light along the
halls along the walls the corridors with loads of love and loads
of hate I carried all the weight of madness now

    When you're aware of sanity you learn of light you know of
dark and then that's it

    Two coppers now more gentle than the docs well used to
violent folk spoke gently those so familiar words there there
hush hush now calm down you're safe again I felt my body
dragging towards a chair my wrists were tight again my wrists
were bound again I just discarded them my spits were dribbles
now and tasted foul were glad to leave my mouth

    A naked bulb a naked me a tree beside my bed a small thin
bed with metal springs another cop another cottage window
almost in the roof I'd heard them tear the room apart to make
a cell of it me for me for I'd become one of the mad folk the
ones you throw away and lock the door and then I heard the
lock unlock I heard a voice so dull and dead the tone of it so
dull and dead it just spat out the words of dread 'she's sec-
tioned now' and that was it forever more the scar of it. the
blight of it the screams of it

    And now I live with it I'm sectioned now for all my life I'm
sectioned now

    In Pat's they scraped the gristle from my brain they scraped
my body too the body I'd forgotten that I had so powerful
was the pain inside my head but there is logic in the mental
madness of it all that's still the case age weakens lots of things
but not the dark old age is cute with pain and even smarter
with the dark it doesn't weaken like the body does the dark

is far too smart for that to try to process thoughts like this is surely walking down the road to madness and insanity

It's cold it's not it's hot it's not

You cry alone you fall alone you fail alone you feel alone alone enough you almost die you see the chaos of your life you see the nights collide with day you see the days collide with nights you see corruption everywhere you feel the shaming everywhere until there's nothing left to do but beg the gods again you beg them now today to speed it up come on just hurry up and take me out of here and then I scream again I feel that shot again I see that face again the devil dressed in white again Miss Divine again and she's on form today I hear her cackle as she screams at me 'I've got you now, Miss Smarty Pants!' 'That's twice today,' she hisses in my ear victorious and loud she ties my hands and slaps my face and walks me down the corridor I see him in there that sick old man who is the maddest of us all and although he scares me half to death I love the man with all my heart I wish I was as brave as him causes chaos all the time torments the staff and shuffles all around the place with only socks upon his feet he hides then runs about scaring all the staff to death and bringing joy to all of us mad folk who do the screaming who shout out differ-ent screams in sheer delight at seeing our jailers running here and running there and calling out for order angry now sud-denly afraid I pushed my face against the glass and wept and wept again I wracked my brain and asked myself how did I do those early years? how did I tiptoe through so many dangerous things? how did I dance through my mother's threats? How did I find the space to run and dance and sing out loud? How did I feel the wonder of it all?

And why the hell can't I do that now? where did I go wrong? where did it go wrong? was it that car that smashed my body up? was it TB jailing me in solitary? was it that woman that woman, that sick and cruel woman who beat me up almost from birth? these are the noises from my past but it's too late now it's far too late and so I fall I give it up surrender all today and die today

I ponder this as Nurse Divine drags from the bright blue glass and walks me towards the firing squad

A Good Psychiatrist

I tried to break my life again, to cut my wrists again. Another ambulance. And here I was again, the Meath Hospital. Again. Lying alone in a big room in a small bed.

A man came in – a good-looking man – and standing at the end of my bed, I watched him slick his hair back with his hand and caught a glimpse of vanity. This man was Dr Anthony Clare.

He said 'Hello' and sat down, telling me he was the head psychiatrist of Dublin town and therefore everything such as cutting wrists would come across his desk. He smiled and held my file up and said, 'Are you aware of the number of times you've cut your wrists?'

'No,' I said.

'Thirty-one,' he answered.

I was surprised. I would have guessed at three, myself.

'This,' he said, 'is the highest number of suicide attempts I've seen since I became a psychiatrist. That's why I noticed it. So talk to me. What's this all about?'

Anthony Clare, I thought. *I've heard of him. A good reputation for psychiatry in Ireland.*

I was kept there for about three weeks and saw him every day. He talked to me in normal tones about depression. No shock, no judgement. And mental illness, he explained to me, was not a thing to be ashamed of.

He cut my stay short, transferring me to St Pat's, a place everybody'd heard about. A madhouse, really. I was terrified. I remember getting out of the ambulance and going through a huge arched door. The building back then was decrepit, old-fashioned, screaming out for help to build its broken walls again. But I felt at home.

This was my first time meeting lunatics.

I would stay in Pat's for weeks and weeks and throughout my life would be admitted many times. They gave me medication in many forms and this was my introduction to pills, which I grew very, *very* fond of down the years.

After good, long conversations with Dr Clare, I was transferred to St Edmundsbury in Lucan. A recovery place. A scaling-down from a public hospital. A big old-fashioned house with lush gardens that were the size of a park all around, completely private, just for us.

Here I came to terms with my depression, almost giving up the fight and knowing that all of this pain was here for life.

Theatre in London

There were lots of theatres in London, lots of actors and lots of directors. It was intimidating at first.

Robert Carrickford helped me to get an agent, and I got a bit of work in small theatres. A lot of the Irish in London then signed on the dole and also worked. I almost did the same myself. A guy called Tony Harris talked me into signing on one day, seducing me with all the money I would get. Twenty pounds or so. There were two queues. He joined one and I joined the other. We were chatting away to each other as we shuffled along. Then the clock on the wall caught my eye. I turned and said, 'I hope they hurry up because I'm going to be late for work.'

Hearing my own words, I was utterly ashamed of what I was doing. I ran from the place and got the Tube out to North Acton to the BBC rehearsal rooms.

I was trying to break into the London acting world, so I got a couple of little jobs – as a glorified extra, really. I made enough to cover the rent of the bedsitter I was in. The Irish actor Kate Binchy's brother David had a big house in Islington. He was an architect and he was doing it up. There was a room on the middle floor and a bathroom that was nearly finished, and I could stay there for tuppence a week.

I got a call to go to the Royal Court, a much-respected theatre, and one I loved. I'd been to see a couple of plays there, and the atmosphere was wonderful. I went to the stage door and asked for a man called David Hare. I was told to go upstairs to the little theatre, that he was waiting there.

I went up and met him. Instantly, I warmed to him, a young lad fresh out of Cambridge. After talking to him for half an hour, I realized he was extraordinary. And indeed I was right. He's now one of the leading playwrights in England, and was recently knighted.

I worked on several plays with him at Royal Court and we became good friends.

When David was casting *Licking Hitler* he phoned me – I was in Dublin – telling me about his latest play. This would be his first foray into film. Not only was he writing the screenplay, but he was also going to direct it. Ambitious, even for a successful theatre director. He said that David Rose, the up-and-coming, much talked-about producer, was producing and that he had already cast Bill Paterson and Kate Nelligan. He was offering me the part of Eileen. I said I'd read the script. He was thrilled. I said I'd phone him later that night.

I was on the second read of the script. It was good. I felt excited that I could be part of it.

A couple of hours later, the phone rang.

'Hello?' I said.

Silence.

'Hello?'

Silence.

'Who's that?'

'It's David,' he whispered.

'Hello,' I whispered back. 'Are you all right?'

'No,' he said. I thought I heard sobbing.

'I can't believe it,' he said. 'David Rose doesn't want you to do the part.' David Rose was the producer.

I was so disappointed I couldn't speak.

'Why?' I said finally.

He explained that the play was about Bletchley Park and all these frightfully upper-class English people. He'd cast Kate Nelligan in the other female part. Kate, of course, was Canadian, and Mr Rose didn't want me to play an English part because I was Irish. He was just uncomfortable with two non-English actors playing English parts.

David apologized profusely. I could feel tears coming, so I said a quick goodbye. I walked around the house for hours, disappointment turning to determination.

How can I possibly get this part?

Slowly, a plan was forming in my head. An hour or so later, I did something that I had never done before and would never do again. I walked around the bedroom practising a posh English accent. My only guide for a posh English accent of the sort I wanted was the film *Brief Encounter*. I held my upper lip to make it stiff. I put a little rubber ball in my mouth and tried to talk in a plummy voice. I did this for an hour or so, then went down to the phone and called David back. I pretended I was a journalist from the *Guardian* who'd got wind of the fact that he was going to make a film about Hitler and asked him to tell me something about it. Who was in it? What was the location?

David was startled the press knew anything about the piece and we had about a five- or six-minute conversation about the drama. Then I thanked him very much and said goodbye.

My hands were shaking with shock that I had done such a thing, but I wasn't finished yet. I phoned him back. 'David,' I said, 'I've just had a journalist from the *Guardian* phoning me up.'

'Oh,' he said, 'she just phoned me too.'

'What did she say?' I asked.

He went on to give an interesting account of our conversation. When he'd finished, I said, with great glee, 'That was me! That was me, David, pretending to be that journalist!'

I was laughing at the whole thing, nervous and delighted, but he went completely silent. He was silent for so long I had to shout, 'David, David, are you there?'

'I am,' he said. I could hear the shock and confusion in his voice. 'Was that really you?' he asked.

'It was,' I said and repeated every word I'd said in the interview.

There was another silence and then he whispered very quietly, 'You've got the part.'

There was a scene in the middle of *Licking Hitler* where my character got the news her brother had been killed in the war. I had to go up to the bedroom and cry my guts out.

Before we shot the scene, David said, 'Brenda, this has to be *awful* crying. I want tears and snots and coughing and everything.'

'Okay,' I said.

He scheduled the scene to be the last one shot before the lunch break. They all set up their tools, then walked out and left me alone in the room to get myself ready. I sat there, pulled up some sad memories, and worked myself into a state until I was bawling crying. It was a fine piece of method acting, worthy of Daniel Day-Lewis.

The door was open. David had heard me sniffling. He tiptoed quietly in and whispered, 'Action'.

I went into a long speech and cried brilliantly. The snots were rolling down my face, which was now bright red. My eyes were swollen. It was an extraordinary performance. It was one take, we broke for lunch, and everyone disappeared, leaving me all alone again.

I was fuming as I sat there cleaning my face. Not wanting to go down for lunch looking like this. I called out for someone to bring me up some food, looking out of the big window.

There was a very long driveway with two curves. I saw a little red dot in the distance, moving. I realized it was a car. I watched it coming up the driveway, a little too fast. It stopped under the entrance, where I couldn't see it. Then up the stairs rushed David Hare, panting and crying. He came into the room with the biggest bunch of flowers, which he gave me with a hug.

'Thank you for the good acting.'

Rape 2

We'd been in Searson's for hours, and I was slightly pissed. I was with Godfrey Quigley, Liz Davis, and James Donnelly, an English actor.

A friend of Godfrey's, James had a mystique about him, because he was very publicly having an affair with the columnist Terry Keane, who was in turn very publicly having an affair with Charlie Haughey, then the minister for finance in the Irish government. All that made him quite exotic. And he was *fun*. Funny, too. Great company. A deep, rich actor's voice carrying a strong upper-class English accent and, with the most impeccable English manners, he was all round what you might call a good egg.

We climbed down slowly from the high stools.

'Time?' Godfrey boomed.

'Six,' chirped Liz adoringly.

'Ah, good, good.'

'We'll get a taxi now.'

'Not at all,' sez I. 'I'll drive you. I'm outside.'

With all the usual mumblings, checkings, dropping things, leaving tips, we skipped out into Baggot Street and piled into my Vauxhall Victor, with its old-style front bench seat and steering wheel gears, and set off for the Gate Theatre, where Godfrey was doing a show.

Godfrey was a big man with big appetites. His voice was even richer and deeper than James's, and the mood was high and happy as we drove down Grafton Street and up O'Connell Street, dropping the two off at the Gate.

Godfrey manoeuvred his way out, straightened himself up to his full height and helped Liz onto the street. Then he kiss-kissed James and me and said, 'See you two later? Groome's?'

'Definitely,' I answered as I turned the car around, saying to James, 'Where next?'

'Let's buy some booze and have a jar at Godfrey's place,' James said. 'I'm staying there, y'know.'

I did know.

'Okay then.'

'Let's get some booze.'

'Oh, there's plenty at the flat. You know Godfrey!'

'Indeed I do!'

We drove slowly back down O'Connell Street, back up Grafton Street, back around the Green, up Leeson Street, and onto Morehampton Road, where Godfrey and Liz had a fabulous basement flat. Finding a parking spot right at the house made us laugh.

He held open the gate and we walked along the long front garden path those houses have, taking it all in and being acutely aware of each other. Did we fancy one another a little? He danced down the three steps to the door under the main steps and, whistling happily, opened it and guided me in. I had been here many times, so I knew my way around.

I heard him behind me, fiddling with bags. I was opening a bottle of wine when he came in, closed the door, and quietly locked it behind him.

This registered.

He took the bottle of wine from me, grabbed a huge brandy glass, and began to pour, all the time telling of his escapades with Godfrey in posh upper-class schools. Handing me the now-brimming-over brandy glass and neatly carrying his rather small shot of whiskey, he took my elbow and quite firmly guided me to the green velvet couch of which Liz was so proud. He didn't exactly push me down, but he did use a firm hand on my shoulder to make me sit down first.

That registered.

He sat beside me – far too close, which made me laugh out loud, get up, and say, 'You got some fags? I have some in the car.'

I saw a pack of Liz's Majors on the arm of the armchair, which I grabbed and opened up. I took one out and offered it to him. Then, remembering he didn't smoke, I proceeded to light up, with every move learned from studying James Dean firing up in *Giant*.

I sensed the tiniest hint of anger and smiled quietly to myself. I threw myself into the big armchair without my drink or an ashtray. Fast as fast, he slid my glass over to me, and then he whipped a saucer from the sink and put it at my feet. He sat cross-legged there and smiled at me. Now he was between the door and me.

That registered.

He started telling some yarn about things that happened during one of his West End hits. It was interesting and funny. Within thirty minutes I was more than halfway down my glass of wine, on my second cigarette, and enjoying myself.

Suddenly the phone rang. I jumped, as it was right beside me, and then burst out laughing as he took it from me, saying, 'Godfrey Quigley residence'. He turned away then, mumbling for a minute or two. Then, saying a loud farewell, he put the phone back on the table. If I had moved a second later I would have missed him quietly taking the phone off the hook before saying gaily, 'More wine?'

That registered.

It crossed my mind to leave, but I felt lazy and mellow and not seriously threatened.

He sat back cross-legged and continued to talk. His English accent was beginning to annoy me. It almost sounded fake at times. I had heard English people in Ireland do that before, put on an extra posh English accent over their normal voice. I had never heard it happen in England.

We talked a bit more. It was getting dull now. But I wanted to go to Groome's later so I lolled about and even poured myself another glass of wine. I was leaning over the kitchen sink to get a clean ashtray when – with the speed of a trapeze artist on the high wire throwing their partner from post to post – he turned and twisted my body, stopping only when he had me trapped between his rock-hard arms, which were leaning on the sink.

His mouth was tight behind my right ear as he said, 'Miss Smarty Pants tonight, are we, eh?'

With that he banged my pelvis so hard against the sink I thought it would break.

'Take your knickers off.'

'No!'

He bashed his right knee up hard against my vagina, shooting pain all through me.

'Take off your knickers!'

I dragged them down slowly, trying to think of a way out. It was his strength that scared me.

I was stepping out of my knickers when he suddenly grabbed my long blonde hair and wrenched me up, flinging my face against the sink.

I could taste blood.

'Take off your skirt.'

I slowly rolled it down. It was at this point he struck like a snake. With sure and strong hands he grabbed each buttock tightly, and then spread them wide. Then he forced his cock right up my bum while I screamed out in pain and shame.

Later he threw me across the arm of the big chair and fucked me so hard he hurt himself.

There are pauses. Blanks.

Did I pass out?

Probably.

I know I fell asleep curled up on the floor because, while half-awake there, I tasted filth as he grabbed my neck and pushed his dirty cock into my mouth, masturbating to orgasm, holding down hard to make sure I swallowed every drop of his filthy sperm, leaving a taste I have never quite managed to wash out of my mouth.

Typewriter and Hospital Work

Séamus S, like Des, hadn't minded at all my playing with his typewriter. He knew how much I loved it. All the bells and the clacking carriage return made me smile. All the fooling around with it made me good enough to be able to type a letter quite well – with two fingers, like all good journalists used to do. But that was enough to get me temporary typing work in London when there were no acting jobs. You signed up with an agency that rented you out to offices in need of a typist. It was all right, but nothing like acting, that amazing life that had fallen into my arms when I wasn't looking for anything at all.

But then sometimes there was no typing work either, and I had to pay the rent. All the thousands of Irish girls in London lived in bedsits in Camden Town or Kilburn. You'd start out in some other girl's bedsit with a mattress on the floor. I did any job I could when there was no typing available, like working at the sweet counter in Woolworths in a white and red uniform with the silliest red hat I'd ever seen. I quickly got fired for eating a whole bar of the latest chocolate that everyone was talking about, a mixture of chocolate and caramel called the Caramac. It was well worth getting fired for.

Out of work again, I went looking for a typing job but there were none. Then, in handwriting on a piece of ordinary white paper stuck to a shop window where you could discover casual jobs, I read: 'cleaner needed for hospital'. I certainly knew about hospitals and I knew about cleaners, the friendliest people in all the hospitals I'd been in. They always seemed happy in their work, so I thought I'd have a go. I phoned the number and got the job over the phone, which surprised me – it was probably my Irish accent – and early the next morning I was standing in the main corridor of University College Hospital in London with a coloured wrap-around apron like a farmer's wife's. I had been given a big aluminium bucket full of water, two mops, a large square of red carbolic soap, and a scrubbing brush the size of a broom. I had also been given another rag – already fairly dirty – that I didn't know what to do with. There were four other women, all Irish. The head porter, Séamus, was also Irish and the men who wheeled the dead bodies out on gurneys were all Irish. As far as I can remember, there were only two Irish doctors out of scores of every nationality you could think of. This band of merry folk, the cleaners and porters, that was so eager to keep everything turning over smoothly, came mostly from rural Ireland.

I thought I knew about hospitals, but cleaning one – scrubbing floors – is very different from being a patient. On that first day, I fell to my knees and onto that dirty dry piece of cloth that had puzzled me before, and began trying to clean the floor. I dipped the scrubbing brush into the water. I rubbed a lot of that square lump of red soap on it, then leaned forward as if adoring Buddha. Then, leaning both hands on the brush, I started scrubbing back and forth, as hard and slow as if in prayer. I worked out a rhythm that wouldn't leave me knackered and was easier on the heels of my hands. The floor tiles were gorgeous. Ten versions of a simple line which fell into combinations of triangles and other intriguing shapes. 'Good woman,' I heard Sister Assumpta, who was in charge of the cleaners, saying. She spoke of how these were beautiful,

beautiful patterns few people saw or searched out, and here I was on my knees right in the middle of so many of these beauties, free to work with them all day long.

But the floors were actually very dirty, so I bent over to scrub each ancient tile of the day's dirt. I could see the other women out of the corner of my eye working hard, scrubbing to their own rhythm. After a few hours I saw how the women cleverly shifted, back and forth, to minimize movement. They chatted easily to each other, sharing laughter. But the work was back-breaking. I found it tough and I was young – half the age of all these other women on their knees. The older ones talked, sometimes to themselves. Sometimes they were praying, freeing their hands now and then to make the sign of the cross, even kissing the crucifixes on their beads before pushing them back into their aprons lest they get caught. Voluntary deprivation. Send a few bob home. That's what you did when you left home and entered the slavery of cleaning England.

Off the corridor, here and there, there were little rooms – holes, really, no doors – where we gathered for our ten-minute breaks to have a cup of tea. We were allowed a break every four hours to do this. There would be an unexpected rush of people leaving their tools neatly beside their buckets, and then scooting to the nearest hole where a massive cauldron of boiling water sat all day. The woman beside me introduced herself. In a half-whisper, she told me her name was Máire and that she was from Donegal. She said that the next break would be ours. When it came she smiled, said, 'c'mon', and led me to the 'tea-room'.

It was crowded, a hunched-up group of women shuffling around the long counter, laughing and whispering as they dragged out pieces of wedding cake, teacake, sponge cake, fairy cakes, and biscuits. Piles of fresh Irish scones smelling as mouth-watering as they always do. There were soggy homemade sandwiches as well, soda bread, ordinary bread.

Everything you could buy in a shop was there, colourful and happy, all bundled together; other women made the tea in the biggest pot I have ever seen in my life. It seemed that within seconds of our break being called, this dreary pit in the wall had been turned into a dazzling, happy place, offering scrumptious food to be stuffed into the mouths of cleaners packed in for their morning break.

Surprisingly, everyone was smiling. Talking quietly to each other. Smoking fags and enjoying their break. They all welcomed me. They were so kind and so thoughtful. Someone handed me the biggest mug I had ever seen with the strongest tea I had ever tasted. Milk and sugar had already been added. Three huge teapots in a row beside several open tins of Barry's Green Label, everything to make a cup of tea as quickly as you could, leaving precious time to lean back against the counter, smoke a fag, and talk quickly and quietly to each other. Here was where you got to know each other. It was overpowering.

I had never been in such a crowd of people in such a small space before. There was something so exciting about this group. They made me feel part of it. I was fully aware of the pain and sorrow they shared, of the need in them to fill their ears with Irish vowels and the comfort to cry their eyes out for whatever private reason while arms tightened around each other, joining their prayers to put the final circle around a ceremony with which no one in the hospital dared interfere. Each one had their story, as did I, but it took me weeks to open up, because I listened every day to the same sad theme: the lonely life of the unwilling immigrant.

Séamus had the big, red, shiny face of a farmer, and his portly body was neatly wrapped up in a navy uniform with a tiny red line around the cuffs and a shiny belt, making him look as smart as the captain of a cruise ship. I knew that, like us all, he was homesick. I spent many happy hours drinking with him in his tiny, unkempt, sad bedsit in Kilburn. He was a really good singer. He even got me to sing with him in the pub next door. In those days, I was inclined to sing when I was drunk. Many's the night I would sing in his arms as an Irish pub, full of Irish folk longing for home, would burst into a rowdy rendering of 'O Danny Boy' as midnight approached.

I worked in the hospital for about four weeks that first time, vowing never to look for a typing job again when out of work, but to always go back to this strong group of Irish immigrants living in an often hostile country, where the minute you opened your mouth, there could be an instant racist response from the English. Don't forget this was when signs in B&Bs still said No Blacks, no Dogs, no Irish.

Looking back on the randomness of getting that job, I saw the dignity in the way my co-workers protected their loved ones at home in Ireland from the truth of the lives they were living in London.

From that group of workers in University College Hospital, I learned a great deal about life. I learned to understand the job, to scorn the people over me and love the ones beside me, to despise the English supervisors, who didn't care if their charges lived or died. You just polished the corridor floors from end to end, and turned around and did it all again.

Brenda in *The Little Mother*.

Meeting Barry

My friend Rosaleen told me that a British director, Barry Davis, was staying at the Gresham Hotel and holding auditions. I didn't care.

'I'll go if I can find a parking space outside the Gresham,' I said.

The parking space was there. It was fate.

Barry was not a handsome man, and he was thirteen years older than me, but he was charismatic and interesting; a well-respected film and television director. Rosaleen and I arranged to bump into him after a show at the Eblana Theatre.

Shortly afterwards, while I filmed a series of plays for Granada Television, directed by him, we fell in love. Barry was an erudite, thoughtful man whose conversation was always wonderfully stimulating.

He was also married with a fucking wife and two fucking daughters.

Love

I could hear the memory fading but definitely not dying as he closed his legs around me, talking lovingly to all of me. I knew what he was doing, had been doing for months and months now.

Each whisper made me love him more. But for all that year or maybe more he'd managed only once to lay his body lovingly on top of mine. Just once. That's all. And we'd both cried like kids, embracing this small step towards the thing I dreaded more than I desired.

To make love to him.

One night I was lying in bed half asleep and he reached across me to get a cigarette when suddenly an awful scream rang out. I jumped and curved into a ball. At once his arms fell all around me and his lips were on my ear while I clung to him and stuttered out the memory of that disgusting man, that dreadful man, who'd pinned me up against the filthy sink and violently and brutally raped me.

Barry held me in his arms until I slept.

I woke up to a sunny day. A pot of coffee and some buttered toast and there he was sitting reading the *Guardian* and all, all of me broke into a million shards of love for him. Then I ran across the room and threw my arms around him, trying desperately not to thank him. Never thank him, he had told me that early on, when I'd explained the rapes to him: 'Never thank me. Gratitude is not the thing I want, Brenda. I want your love and gratitude demeans that. Despite the damage that's been done to you, I can feel your love. We'll get there,' he whispered. 'We will.'

He threw on his beautiful tweed jacket, kissed my mouth, and said, 'I'll see you in Paddy's at six.'

And he was gone.

I ran to the window and watched him walk all the way to the end of the street, wondering again, would he come back to me that night?

Coronation Street

What can I tell you about my gig on *Coronation Street*? I'm smiling just writing about it. Back then, being on *Coronation Street* was the coolest thing that could possibly happen to any actor. For an Irish actress trying to make a career for herself in Britain, it was unheard of. I think I was the first Irish actor to be in the series. I played the nurse who delivered Deirdre Barlow's first child, and because this was such a big television occasion, and the whole of England was waiting for the delivery of this baby, just by being a part of that fictional birth, I am still remembered.

Kitchen sink drama had changed everything about television programming, and was having a massive influence on all the younger writers. On everyone. It changed theatre and television for ever. Out of it came all those amazing writers. Alan Bennett. Arnold Wesker.

From *Coronation Street*'s first ever episode, the public had been mesmerized. When it was on, the streets emptied. *Everyone* watched it. Not everyone had televisions at the time. Those who didn't would run to one of the houses that had a set, making sure not to miss it.

Once on the set, I was rendered speechless because here were people like Peter Adamson, Julie Goodyear, and Jean

Alexander. One of the characters, Ena Sharples, was played by a brilliant actor called Violet Carson. Ena Sharples was a fat, cranky lady who never took her hairnet off, and was always grumpy and unlikeable.

Suddenly needing a pee, I went out to the bathroom. As I was peeing, I heard some wonderful piano music. At first I thought it was on the radio, but then I realized it was live, and it was near me. I went to see if I could find it. I found an open door and looked in.

A beautifully carved out little set of steps led to a small dais with a magnificent, highly polished grand piano standing gracefully alone. And there, also sitting alone and equally elegant, playing an easily recognizable passage from Beethoven's Fifth Symphony, was Ena Sharples. There she was, in her full glory, her back as straight as a rod, her eyes closed, away in a world of her own, playing the most sublime music in the world.

I could not speak, so gorgeous was the sight of this strange, fat, old lady dressed in the dowdy clothes of Ena Sharples. I watched her moving hands – her too-graceful, too-smooth hands, with long, elegant fingers that skipped with delicate speed and light over the firefly dance stretch in that piece and on to the sweet ending. Her head was back. Her eyes were closed. Her face was peaceful.

My eyes had tears in them as she carefully came down the little steps. She spotted me and came over for a chat, but when she saw how the music had moved me she burst out laughing – a huge, loud, happy laugh.

'Hard to beat, isn't he?' she said.

Trying not to cry, I was about to answer her, when a voice behind shouted: 'Brenda Fricker! You're welcome, welcome, welcome to *Coronation Street*!'

I turned around and saw a woman called Pat Phoenix, who played the character of Elsie Howard in the show, walking towards me with her arms spread out.

Pat Phoenix at that time was the sex symbol of England. She was worshipped, and with good reason. Her personality filled the room. She was a big lady in every way. Big bosoms. Big bum. Big laugh. To meet her in the flesh was overpowering. She threw her arms around me, almost knocking me to the ground.

She could see the state that I was in, so she linked my arm.

'Come on,' she said to Mrs Carson. 'It's Brenda's first day. Let's take her to have a cup of tea.'

Mrs Carson linked my other arm, and off we went to have tea in the canteen in Granada Studios.

I can't remember much about the tea, but I can remember everything about the walk.

All the way home on the bus I was on a complete high, knowing that something astonishing had happened to me during my rehearsals for the most popular soap opera in the world.

And nobody knew that except Violet Carson, Pat Phoenix, and me.

They Flew Along the Tiled Corridor (Miscarriage)

They flew along the tiled corridor, shaky little rubber wheels on each corner of the stretcher making loud, ugly noises. The inside of my brain?

The ambulance men were experienced and quiet. They spoke softly, as if they were giving me a guided tour of the building. Little did they realize that I knew exactly where I was. Little did they know that, not six months before, I had been scrubbing the tiles on the very floor I was now being wheeled along. The irony made me smile but, immediately, I pulled my legs up to my shoulders and subdued a scream against the pain that darted through the whole of my body. I stifled a cry for what the pain might mean.

Now we were waiting for a lift. The pain got worse, making me grab my thighs and bury my head in the thin pillow on the stretcher. Tears were pouring down my face when, from nowhere, a hand gently stroked my head with a tenderness I have not felt since. I folded my arm back awkwardly to touch the source and felt the young, soft skin of one of the ambulance men. He was twenty, maybe twenty-one, barely a man.

I screamed weakly with the pain, but with a desperate gratitude for this magnificent gesture of simple kindness. What did Tennessee Williams say about the kindness of strangers? I dragged the young man's hand to my lips and kissed it, knowing there would be little, if any, kindness in the hours to come. My heart was breaking, but I had the imprint of his hand on my lips as the men opened the doors.

I knew all about the stretching of time. Now the pain was making it stretch. Rapture could do it too. So could memory. We seemed to go through an endless stream of double doors, which were loudly pulled open as we flew along. I knew what was going on. I had often ridden on this particular roundabout. There was no mystery here at all. I had had three full dress rehearsals, or was it four? All-over tired as I was, I more or less knew the way it ended. I was acutely aware that my life would never ever be the same again. That I would be shaped by the next few hours.

The men wheeled me into one of the operating theatres in University College Hospital in London. My future was going to be filled with this failure and I could physically feel my heart breaking as the men rolled me from the stretcher onto the operating table. I managed to keep my eyes open as they swept me across. They quietly said goodbye, and the younger one leaned over to whisper, 'Good luck, Brenda. You'll be fine.' His kindness was all I had and I clung to it as if to retain my sanity, as the God I didn't believe in allowed me an escape and my body fainted – briefly – into a welcome, comforting oblivion.

Then hands put something under my bum to raise it up and dragged my legs apart as if to stuff me for Sunday lunch.

'Knock her out, old boy,' I heard the surgeon whisper. 'It's a bit of a mess down here.'

Before I knew it, that beautiful half-ball-shaped hollow silver thing was smashed onto my face and I went somewhere happy.

I awoke on my side. All the skin in my vagina was stinging. I was moving around, trying to soothe the sting, when my eye caught a kidney tray with blood dribbling out of it. I raised my hand and brought the tray down beside me to clean it, or at least wipe it down. I jumped back in horror when I saw what was in it: a human doll. He was perfectly formed, with toes, ears, and a nose almost too small to see. He was wet with blood and slime but that wasn't what turned me cold. This was my child, I suddenly realized. My foetus. My little boy.

My body jumped up and I heard my voice screaming at the doctor standing beside my bed: 'Save him! Save him! Save him!'

I slapped the doctor's fat face as hard as I could. I punched his stomach, screaming at him to save my son. I spat at him and kicked his shins before three or four nurses grabbed my arms and held me very hard, police-style, hurting me. I kicked and screamed as they forced me back onto the trolley and pulled the anaesthetic back onto my face, knocking me out again.

Royal Court

I was working at the Royal Court again, in the little theatre upstairs. This was my third time there. It's the theatre where I first felt the real thrill of acting. It was there more than anywhere – even the National Theatre – that I felt I was beginning to understand what it is to be an actor. I developed a confidence in the craft while still knowing the pleasure and the pain of it. I still feel those things when I hear the curtain going up or when I hear someone shouting 'Action!'

The play I was doing was *The Pleasure Principle*, written by Snoo Wilson and directed by David Hare, two of the hottest young men in town. David was tall, gangly, and shy, and sometimes scary. Snoo was tall and shy and never scary. My inferiority complex about having virtually no education disappeared when I was with these men. I don't think they had a clue that I was drinking in every word they spoke or wrote but if they did, they certainly never made me feel uncomfortable. I was nervous and self-conscious around them. I was way out of my league in their company. They were so well-mannered that you'd be fooled into thinking we were old friends. They made me feel so *present*. Their enthusiasm was infectious. Their understanding and questioning of everything around them impressed me. They were so very young. Boys, really. They were the bright boys, the bright young boys who wanted, with ease, to completely change the world around them.

We had broken for lunch and as it was a lovely summer day I'd agreed to meet Barry in the pub beside the theatre, but when I got there it was crammed, full to the doors, so I cast my eye over the little tables outside and spotted a couple of empty seats at the table in the far corner. Two guys were sitting there but the other two seats were empty, so I wormed my way in and around the crowded tables and asked the men if the seats were free. They shot up like toy soldiers saying yes, yes, yes, of course yes, please sit down, let me take your papers. I smiled at their good manners. True English gentlemen. I sat down, put my script on the table, and took a couple of deep breaths to cool myself.

I was trying to catch the waiter's eye when the thin man stood up and asked, 'Would you like a drink?' He had a beautiful voice, a beautiful head, a beautiful face.

'No, no,' I said. 'What would *you* like to drink?' The smile did it.

'A pint please.'

The other man was very different: plump, red-cheeked, and happy, with a huge smile and fabulous teeth.

'We're all Guinness babies then!' he said.

I laughed and opened up my script to read it through again. A tip Barry gave me: 'Read your script twenty, thirty, forty, fifty times. Then read it one more time before you go to bed.'

The drinks finally arrived, well-poured pints of Guinness that brought smiles to all our faces. We did the usual chit chat. We introduced ourselves. The plump man was Howard and the thin man was Sam. The ice was broken as we raised our glasses with the usual words: 'Cheers! Good health! *Sláinte.*'

Eh? It was the thin man who said *sláinte,* not me. Aha!

I smiled across at him. 'Are you Irish?' I asked.

'I am,' he answered smiling. Instantly, we were friends. Seeing the script, Howard asked if I was working at the Court.

'I am,' I said.

'Snoo's play?'

'Exactly,' I said proudly.

'And David's directing, yes?' the thin man asked.

'Yes, yes,' I said eagerly, delighted and proud to be exactly where I was in my life at that exact moment.

The fat man laughed with joy. 'You're one lucky lady,' he said. 'They are two of the most talented people working in the theatre today.'

Proud as Punch, I said, 'I know! I've worked with David before and I think he's a genius too.'

'Yes,' the fat man said.

'You're with two serious young talents,' the thin man said.

'I know, I know.'

I smiled up at him as I eagerly babbled out every single detail about how astonishingly great it felt to just be in the same room as them. I blushed again as I boasted to them, then blushed again in an apology for ranting about how David was picking up the weak parts in the writing and how indeed they let the actors contribute to every part of the production, which, of course, gave us a great feeling of inclusion and confidence. I rattled on about how most writers – particularly the ones who were still alive – didn't have the first clue about actors and their needs and their contribution. David was not like that at all, but I had worked with writers who'd have a fit if you changed one word! We all three laughed at my obvious frustration.

These were two impressive men who were different as chalk and cheese. Their passion excited me. I laughed, not wanting to leave their company.

'When's the first night?' the thin one asked.

'Oh God … in two weeks, I think. Maybe three.'

'Well, well,' he laughed, a hint of retribution in his tone. 'What method do you use to be ready for that all important first night?'

I suddenly felt sick.

What method? Before I'd only ever heard the word 'method' linked with 'Brando'. I didn't fully understand the meaning of it, other than knowing it was a technique of acting. Suddenly the good feeling I had disappeared and I felt so ignorant and threatened that I couldn't answer them. I blabbered out some nonsense about having been a journalist with the *Irish Times*, sinking deeper and deeper into mortification as I heard my own words burying me. The thin man quietly laughed, saying I'd made an interesting leap from journalism to acting and how he knew the *Irish Times* well, knew it to be an excellent paper, a paper of record, and one he made a point of reading every day. I began to really like this gaunt-looking man. He seemed quite bright and was putting me at ease so graciously.

We were on our second drink when I saw Barry looking around for me. I stood up and waved at him – over-excited, as the stout was kicking in. He saw me and smiled. My heart missed a beat and I felt my cheeks go red. Sometimes I loved him more than others, and this was one of them.

Barry was weaving his way through the little tables, nodding a couple of times to people he knew. As always, he was clutching a big bundle of papers to his chest, refusing every morning to use either of the briefcases he had at home.

I was fussing around, pulling the fourth chair out from under the table. But as he drew closer my heart dropped at the expression on his face. Was it anger? At *me*? Oh my God, please, please no. Don't let him bring one of his angry, awful moods to this table where I've been having the best time. Then *I* became angry. His bad moods were so destructive they harmed me, harmed him, harmed our relationship.

I started to stand up, ready for battle, but by the time Barry had reached our table I could see he was flustered. That was not like him at all. What's wrong? I thought.

As I stood up he grabbed my arm, almost knocking over the pints. He took my hand and walked me back towards the main entrance, whispering something in my ear that I couldn't hear. With every step I took, I was getting more and more confused.

Pushing his face against mine, he hissed, 'Don't you know who that is?'

'Who?' I asked.

'For God's sake Brenda, you were sitting beside Samuel Beckett! And that's Howard Brenton beside him!'

Samuel Beckett, one of greatest playwrights in the world. So much so that Barry was afraid to sit down beside him.

Turning the Heel

I trotted off to M&S and bought two enormous Aran sweaters, the ones I'd seen the Clancy brothers wear. As I made my way to the till I felt the tears welling up from nowhere. I could see my mother sitting by the fire, head gently to one side, her knitting needles clicking in a rhythm so clean you'd have no problem dancing to it as she effortlessly made her way along the stitches. Lift one here, drop one there, to get to the serious test of turning the heel.

They walked from far and near to give her their unfinished socks: 'Would you turn the heels for me, Bina? They're for big Seán. You know yourself. The size of him.' She'd happily take them in, finish them off, dampen them down, tear up a brown paper bag, and place it over them then iron them.

I put the Aran sweaters down and ran out of the shop and walked along Oxford Street with tears pouring down my cheeks. Aran sweaters were the uniform of the emigrant.

Oh fuck, all this crying. What's wrong with me? *I* don't have to fucking emigrate. Unlike those boys and girls forced to leave, some never to see their homes again.

Gránia had been forced by our mother along that road, denied a third-level education because Bina refused to let her go to Trinity College Dublin as it was a Protestant university.

Unless she went to UCD, the very Catholic UCD, she wasn't going to any university at all. And Gránia wouldn't budge. It broke my heart to see her pain. To hand her towels to wipe the tears that she cried and cried till she was spent. She fell into my young arms and slept while I held her tight till she woke up.

She was damaged for the rest of her life, damaged in so many ways. A bright and beautiful young girl broken in the name of God. Another victory for the Catholic Church. The Church meant more to our mother than the education of her child.

Gránia woke and kissed my brow.

'I love you.'

I never saw her cry again.

She died at sixty-eight thinking she was a failure. She told me all this before she died. She died a drunk. An alcoholic. A functioning alcoholic, which meant she wouldn't drink in front of me, nor would she have any alcohol in the house when I was there, so there would be no need for me to demean her by going around the house looking for hidden bottles of gin.

Brenda and her husband Barry having fun
while drunk in Hyde Park.

Books

I'm a reader. I read as many books as I can. I have a complex
about not having finished school and not being as educated
as every fucking person around me. I read all the books that I
should have read when I was young, and more.

When I was with Barry he encouraged my reading and
would discuss books when I finished them. I read all the books
my father should have been bringing me when I was in hospital: *Peter Pan*, *Macbeth*, *Moby Dick*, *Wuthering Heights*,
and everything by Ernest Hemingway and William Trevor –
mostly those paperbacks with the penguin on the front. Barry
never *told* me to read anything; he just brought the books
home and left them lying around. Barry had graduated from
King's College London with a degree in English, he'd been a
teacher, and he had run for Parliament. An interesting man,
and he was now guiding me.

Those are probably the only books I have read over and
over again. They have become like bibles to me. They have
helped me as an actor; they have helped me in my life.

America

'I've been offered a job in New York,' Barry said casually.

I swung around in my chair saying, 'What?! Say that again?'

'And I'm thinking of taking it,' he said.

My heart missed a beat and I caught my breath and spat out at him, 'Thinking about WHAT? For God's sake, man, will you pull yourself together and listen to yourself? You're THINKING of taking it? Get on that phone to Harvey Whatshisname and tell him yes, yes, yes, we're all packed up and ready to go. I can't think of anything more exciting than going to New York!'

I hugged him tight and kissed his neck.

'I agree,' he said.

We were both working at the BBC so our days were full and long: me acting, him directing. I was dying to talk about America, to ask what play he was going to do, where we would live. I had phoned my lifelong friend Anne Mulligan, who lives in New York, and we laughed with the excitement of perhaps seeing each other again.

I had known Anne since I was a baby. My mother and her mother were best friends and Anne and I had been wheeled out in prams together, so we also became best friends. Now we were in our thirties.

I didn't tell Barry I had phoned her, but two weeks went by and when he hadn't mentioned it again, I began to think there might be something wrong. I had learned early on in my marriage that there was a need sometimes for me to be wily.

I was home before Barry that night and had time to cook a *paella*. This was not a regular occurrence. I've never been interested in or good at housework or cooking. Gránia wasn't interested in housework but was a brilliant cook. The only food I knew anything about was hospital food. Three meals a day handed to me on a tray. Dull as ditchwater.

He came into the kitchen, telling me he had been asked to do a play in the Long Wharf Theatre in New Haven, Connecticut. His friend Arvin Brown was the artistic director there. He had asked Barry before to work there, but Barry had been busy.

This was different. I could go with him to America! I was eaten up with excitement and plans, not stopping to think about the realities.

That night we got drunk and happy. He hugged me tight and whispered, 'My pocket, my love, my pocket.'

Joining in the happy mood, I said, 'Let's go to the pub.'

'My pocket,' he kept repeating, laughing in my ear. I pulled back and saw his face beaming with happiness. I had not seen him like this since our early courting days. Delighted with his mood I reached into his breast pocket and pulled out a long brown envelope folded in half. Nervously, I took out one piece of beautiful heavy cream parchment and slowly began to open it.

Unable to contain his excitement, he leaned over my shoulder, and read out loud as if announcing world peace: 'This is an American work visa for me. You can get one later, but this tells me that I can work in the USA for one year from 1

January 1976 to 1 January 1977. You can come with me on a holiday visa, so get your passport updated.'

I froze on the spot, stared into his eyes, saw the joy of his success, his achievement, his chance.

His arms were stretched out wide now, his face was like a clown's, all his muscles stretching into an unpractised smile. We danced and danced around the house, laughing like little kids: 'New York, New York, here we come!' We danced out through the door, across the road, and down three blocks or so and straight into the bar, and he called out, 'Drinks on us! Please join us in a toast to happiness and more drunken nights!'

And I can say that that was among the best drunken nights I ever had in all our sixteen years together. And, believe me, there were many, as this all happened in the seventies, when everyone was in some stage of inebriation at all times and nobody cared, nobody frowned, nobody judged, you just got drunk.

I don't remember much about the next four weeks other than getting my passport updated and phoning Anne to tell her the good news. She said to bring proper winter clothes, as New York would be bitterly cold and although everywhere was centrally heated I would need warm clothes to walk the sidewalks of New York City.

There it was! My first taste! The 'sidewalks'. That Irish immigrant song flooded through my veins and I could hear my mother's shy voice singing it quietly to herself:

Boys and girls together, me and Mamie O'Rourke
Tripped the light fantastic
On the sidewalks of New York.

It all became too much. I sat down and just let the tears flow. A song strong enough to break a grown man's heart and leave a girl like me spent upon the floor.

Singing in the Pubs in America with Anne

I'd had another row with Barry and although Anne and John only had one bedroom, they'd let me come and sleep on their silver velvet sofa in the sitting room. John – who was a famous footballer with the Jets – had said that I could stay with them for a while.

Anne and I were in our early thirties, and Anne had just had her first baby, a girl called Erin. We were hanging around one evening and I was strumming on John's guitar. Anne was singing along and the mood was happy. Suddenly John said, 'Hey, girls! I've got an idea. A couple of friends of mine own a pub over on Third Avenue. It's an Irish pub – a singing pub, I think. Why don't we all go over some night and you two can sing songs there?'

As horrified as I was, Anne was over the moon.

'That'd be a great idea!' she said.

I laughed it off and forgot all about it. A few nights later, Anne came home saying they had got a babysitter and that we were off to Paddy's Pub on Third Avenue.

With the guitar stuck beside me in the back seat, we drove quickly to Third Avenue, my hair blowing in the wind, and Anne's blowing in my face.

Anne had pulled me aside the night before and told me that she knew all the words to a song and that we should rehearse it. It was three simple chords, A, D and C – all of which were taught to me by Andres Segovia, when I lived in Spain – so we'd well be able to do it. Anne could sing. I couldn't. But, to my amazement, I found I had a talent for harmonizing, which suited us perfectly.

Anne was tall, with perfect proportions. She had pale blonde hair, beautiful small blue eyes, perfect white teeth, and a smile to die for. In our teens, we all used to stare at her when we were changing our clothes to get ready for our performances in the Father Mathew *feis*. She had *huge* breasts, which fascinated those of us who had none. We admired them as we stuffed cotton wool down our bras, in our pathetic attempt to fool the boys. How did her back manage to stay straight when she was walking? But she had great deportment.

She said they were murder on her back but she carried them beautifully, dressing cleverly, revealing just enough to make the young men drool as they pushed their hands quickly into their pockets in case their excitement was visible. All of them drank in this stunning woman, who was the sexy half of the act. And there I was, a plain enough girl enjoying the whole idea of singing together in this mad Irish pub.

I pulled over a long-legged stool and sat on it. Smiling at all the Aran sweaters surrounding me, I draped the guitar strap over my shoulder and waited for our turn to come. As usual, Anne took total control.

'This is what we'll do, Brenda. We'll wait until they quieten down. You play the chord of C, I'll hum along in tune, then we'll pause, and then we'll start the song.'

Gazing straight at me, Anne nodded her head, an agreed sign to begin.

Jesus, why the fuck am I here? Is there any way of getting out of this, I wondered.

But then I heard Anne's clear voice singing aaah to check the key. There was no coming back then. As instructed, I played the chord of C, and as we'd done before, she broke easily into song, singing sweetly and enjoying herself. That made it easy for me to strike the chords and accompany her.

The chorus was in A, which I always got wrong, but Anne had solved this by giving me a clever little harmony. If she or I went wrong, we just bluffed until we found ourselves on the right track again. We could have sung the same song half a dozen times as the whole pub joined in, all the drinkers drunk and the whole place swaying. The drunks singing quietly and missing home. The mood changed now, reflecting immigrant loneliness, the real thing.

John's friend, the owner, came out with an empty biscuit tin, which he passed around the crowd, looking for dollars as a mock fee. Roaring with laughter, he handed us the box, which I took.

'What do we do with this?' Anne said.

'Give it back!' I said.

We were astonished that these people would hand over their hard-earned money to us. We went around and tried to give it all back. The whole scene became chaotic as many of them insisted on us keeping it. In the end, Anne just left it behind the bar to pay for drinks for everyone so that that they would get their money back in in some form or other.

After that, we got a bit cocky and played in a few pubs up and down Third Avenue. I drank Guinness all the time. Anne and John didn't drink, but unlike many abstainers, they were able to get drunk on the laughter as the night went on.

I had moved from glasses, half pints, to pints of the beautiful black nectar and handled them, to everyone's surprise, extremely well. Three pints induced intense listening to others. Four pints got me humming along. Five pints made me get up and recite a poem, usually Yeats. He never failed to bring strong men to their knees. It made them try to remember the words and join in because they had all learned these poems at school. I knew that the fifth pint was expansive, and that was my limit. At six pints, I started to hug and kiss everybody. Seven pints, and I was on the floor.

On those evenings, after our set, Anne and I would go outside and lean against the wall, laughing. Our voices would reach the sky and echo back at us. Anne found the whole thing so funny she'd sink down on her hunkers and shake all over, squeaking out a plea to stop stop stop ooooops, she'd actually wet herself from laughing. And I would laugh even louder, because that's what friends do.

Brenda with her sister Gránia and father Des on her right,
her niece Billy and nephew Chimo on her left.

Paul Newman

The Real Housewives of Beverly Hills. I watch it every night before I go to sleep.

I lived that life for a while after winning The Prize.

But back in 1977, Barry was working in the small and much-respected Long Wharf Theatre in Connecticut.

I was sitting in the bar having an end-of-day drink with Barry when a voice said smoothly into my ear, 'You have a lovely still quality on the screen.'

I turned to thank the man whose voice it was and came nose to nose with Paul Newman.

It's true, his eyes were an intense blue. His charm was real and sexiness just oozed out of him.

Helpfully, Barry explained that he'd seen a film we'd done together. *The Little Mother*, directed by Barry himself for Granada Television. The reason we had met. Paul Newman had, he said, been very impressed.

Bina Sick

The doctor told us she had a brain tumour. The three of us sat there, unable to comprehend. She was in the Meath, the family favourite. Where else?

The visit was over; the doctor indicated this as he rose to leave, saying that someone would be in with us in a minute to help explain. I don't know how long we sat there in silence, our minds in turmoil.

Des slowly put his head into his hands and my heart broke for him. Now would he feel guilty? Guilty for ignoring her for most of their marriage? Was he even aware of having the thing he'd wanted all his life, solitude? Now he had it.

And what about me? All the lies I had told her. The hundreds of times I had laughed at her, belittling her.

Gránia walked over to the window overlooking the car park. I just sat there, drawing any bit of strength I could from anywhere I could to cover up the guilt that was overwhelming me. I tried desperately not to cry. Nothing this serious had happened to us before.

Suddenly we didn't know each other. We were not a unit anymore. Instead, we were caught up in our own versions of death, one guarding the other with a strange new love for Bina. The sadness in that little room was crushing.

I heard Des make a small noise and realized that he was weeping for his Bina.

I could see him struggling to keep calm. My heart was breaking as I stood there in the middle of the room, not knowing what to do to help. Then Gránia turned from looking out of the window, went across to him, and put her arms around his shaking shoulders. He grabbed her body and grunted out the strangest sounds. His hands were gripping her thighs, grabbing onto her dress like a drowning man. It was terrible to watch. I pulled him close and laid his head upon her shoulder so he would know that he was safe. I gently stroked his balding head while mumbling some words to him. It would be the first time and last time we would all share love.

I stepped back, realizing that the intimacy in Gránia and Des's embrace belonged to both of them. I was alone and I knew it, beaten down by this dreadful thing. Knowing this, I killed the scream rising in my throat. And then there was silence. Somehow none of this involved me. Gránia reached an arm out, inviting me to lean on her and Des. Then, carefully, I guided him back to the chair I had just vacated.

Years later, I would confide in a friend that all I felt was pity. I felt he was emotionally empty and had always been like that. I just thanked God for having given me back then the strength to close my mouth and let the two of them share a strange and awkward love.

Let it be, I thought, *don't challenge it.* And so I stretched my arms around the awkward shape of grief and was surprised to find some solace there, although there was no chance to say, 'I'm sorry', 'good luck', 'goodbye'.

This private moment was broken by two nuns coming in to tell us that it was time to leave that room and go upstairs where Bina was laid out and ready to view. She was still alive but had only hours left.

The blood drained from Des's face. He staggered against the wall, gasping for breath, indicating that we should go ahead.

Reluctantly, we obeyed.

I was aware of the evil in me now. How, even now, even in this moment, this singular tragic moment, the evil jealousy of my father's love for Gránia interrupted for a moment any grief or loss or love I might have felt for Bina and her strange love for me.

Completely overcome by the time I got upstairs, I sat down on a chair.

'Here's the room,' the nun whispered, as she ushed my father in, whispering to us, 'Give them a few minutes on their own.'

My mind was blank now. There was not a single thought in it as I waited there alone. Later (an hour? half?), Gránia was there, beckoning to one of the nuns.

'I'm very sorry for your loss,' the nun said in a voice so full of love it caught me off guard. I swayed a bit and thanked her.

'Which is the last faculty to go?' Gránia asked.

'We get asked that question a lot,' the nun replied. 'Ninety per cent of doctors believe that hearing is the last faculty to go.'

There was a moment of complete silence.

'Where has Des gone?' I asked.

'He's gone home,' Gránia whispered, putting her hands on my shoulders. 'He's gone home. He can't face her dying, he said. He just can't cope with this bit, Brenda. Don't judge him. As we both know, he's weak about some of life's tests.'

How could she know these things? She had always been closer to him than I had. She had always been difficult and challenging with him. Did he like that more than the unconditional love *I* had for him? Well, after all, I had been my mammy's little doll. Gránia had been the serious, questioning one, head girl in her school in Balla. Sports captain too. Top of the class. A year ahead yet always first in everything. Nearly five years older than me, she was many years ahead of me in her ability to converse about any subject. She read the *Irish Times* every day and she understood it. They'd help each other out with the difficult Crosaire crossword puzzle while I struggled with the Simplex. She had always been better company for Des, more rounded.

Of course he let her see him running away from tragedy so deep he couldn't face it. He'd never let *me* see something like that.

The nun came back. 'She's ready,' she whispered.

Terrified, I threw my body against Gránia's and wept on her shoulder. The nun allowed this for five minutes? Ten? Then Gránia gently pulled my head back until my face was in front of hers.

'We are going in now,' she said. 'Forget every bad thing she has ever done. You go to the right-hand side and I will stay on her left, and we will keep whispering "I love you" into her ears.'

We, two adult daughters, kneeled on either side of our dying mother, each saying 'I love you' into an ear, so that Bina might know she was loved as she took her final breaths.

Afterwards, the surgeon explained to us that the tumour was a highly unusual one and that he'd like to use it in his teaching, to show it to his students. Shocked at this idea, as one we both said no. Then Gránia asked him how long the tumour could have been there.

'It could have been there all her life,' he said.

'Would this have caused violent behaviour?' she asked.

'Maybe,' he replied.

Des looked so weak when we got home. He couldn't look us in the eye.

Casualty/Bristol

Cassie, my agent, had recommended that I meet a TV producer called Geraint Morris. I had a few drinks with him in the BBC bar in Shepherd's Bush, which was the best place in the world to have a drink and enjoy the company of interesting people. Anybody who was anybody and anybody who was nobody and everybody who was anybody drank in the BBC bar. And everyone was pissed. It was a very big room with a curving counter, behind which were three or four young lads serving a room that was always loud with people hunched in small groups. You'd see small groups from each production leaning in towards one another over the small tables.

Every time I write about 'everyone being pissed', I stop and question it. One of my wonderful friends left alive: my fellow Ena Burke graduate, costume designer Joan Bergin is a non-drinker, and I asked her if my memory was fooling me, or if it was just because Barry and I were hard drinkers that I remember the whole era and all its participants being outrageously drunk. She reassured me that I'm absolutely right.

But even though it's true, I'm not trying to make it seem seedy, because it wasn't like that at all. It was exciting, productive, creative, and successful. The drama productions at the BBC were known for their high standards (challenged only by Granada TV, which for a few golden years produced great plays and series that we actors were queuing up for, in the hopes of getting an audition). But the Beeb remained the champion.

I was always nervous going in on my own, but I soon saw Geraint Morris waving. I made my way over, hugged him, and sat down. His face was great. Bright smiling eyes. Great eyebrows. He was a quiet man with a beautiful Welsh accent. As we chit-chatted the initial necessary small talk, I was aware of the good easy air around us.

We talked for a while, enjoying our well-poured pints and then he broached the reason I was there. I was rehearsing a play called *Lavender Blue* at the National Theatre.

He jumped straight to the point: 'Brenda, the BBC is going to shoot six episodes of a hospital drama.'

My heart fell a little with thoughts of *Emergency Ward 10*, an awful series that had come out of Granada few years before.

Reading my mind he smiled and said, 'I see your hesitation but, Brenda, this is going to be a fast-moving, documentary-style drama.'

Now I was interested.

He'd already cast just one actor. 'Who?' I asked.

'Derek Thompson,' he said.

'Aghh, Derek!' I cried. 'I'm working with him right now. What a great choice! A wonderful actor!'

He explained to me how the show would consist of six or eight hour-long episodes, all shot on one camera. It would start shortly after I finished at the National. Here it was again, the right job at precisely the right time. If I'd sat down years before and planned out the perfect steps for my career it would have been exactly the career I was having.

And I was now about to accept a full year's work for the BBC!

Brenda, acting.

Des Dies

When Des was dying, we were all standing around his hospital bed, feeling lost.

Gránia's partner, John, had come up from Galway. He too was a drunk. He too adored Des. As we each handled our grief in different ways, John had disappeared on a pub crawl around Dublin.

My niece Billy was by the bed. As usual, she was composed. Observing. Half-listening to something on her stylish Walkman. The sound of Des's death-rattle was ringing around the room. None of us could move. He was drowning in his own phlegm, gasping for one final clean breath of air. His face was a study in agony.

I ran out and grabbed the first doctor I saw and begged him to pour poison down my father's throat. To kill him. To stop his agony.

Back in the room, I noticed Billy taking her headphones off and I could just make out ... Beethoven, was it? The Sixth Symphony. Des's favourite music. She leaned across his body and, with such grace and kindness, she lowered the headphones over his head. The two padded earpieces sat gently, and – as no drug in that hospital could have achieved – I saw pain drain from that beautiful face as peace fell over him.

I often think of what Billy did that day. It remains one of the loveliest acts of kindness I've ever seen. I don't have that natural and spontaneous sort of kindness.

Gránia had phoned the Purcell family in Tipperary earlier in the day, telling Johnson that Des was dying. Johnson Purcell, Des's best friend, and his wife, Mary, arrived a few hours later. I watched the blood drain from his ruddy farmer's face.

'Oh no,' he groaned, leaning on the wall for balance.

After eighteen hours with Des, I was exhausted.

'You should go home and have a shower and come back,' Gránia whispered.

I did.

Half an hour later, on my way back, I had to go past that rugby hotel on Leeson Street and reached a thick crowd of fans up for the match and causing a dreadful traffic jam. I sat in my car for fifteen minutes. Ignoring the Gardaí, I inched my way through the crowd then rushed on back to the hospital.

I parked the car, got out, and saw Gránia standing on the steps.

Immediately, I knew Des was dead.

Brenda's sister Gránia in her later years.

Brenda's mum Bina with her first grandchild, Billy.

Method Acting

Everything I learned as an actor I learned from well-rounded people who were joyful at the adventure of working together. Who enjoyed the initial fun and games, then moved on to the terror of being serious and then ran from that to the nearest pub to drink good pints of Guinness as we went through the whole nights and days cycle again.

The really talented ones were *not* the method actors who, in my experience, interrupted every other actor's way of working, as they trampled their way towards a performance, wounding the ordinary players like me. I only came up against it half a dozen times and I learned nothing but self-preservation from any of them. I would rather live in penury than go through all that nonsense again.

But I was lucky – I was *blessed* – to have the honour to be allowed to study, to discuss, to absorb lessons from great actors like Paul Scofield and Dirk Bogarde. These men had humour at their fingertips. They were good team members and respected their fellow actors, including the people who had just one line. There were people like Colin Blakely, Jimmy Ellis, Dave Allen, Susan Fleetwood, Ray McAnally, and Maureen Toal, to name some of the best.

I learned everything I know about acting, and an awful lot I didn't know about living, from those generous people, with whom I had fun beyond fun, while all the time they were drilling me with a hardcore, in-your-face discipline that has been the centre of my acting ever since. Over and over they guided me to a place where I, and I alone, was responsible for giving a good or bad performance.

Method actors, however, hinder me.

I respect every actor's method, as long as it doesn't interfere with mine. But sadly, there are actors whose method definitely interferes with mine. It's as simple as that.

Method actors get into the costume and put on the accent or whatever is required, and they go onto the set. They stay in their character all day long. So if they're playing someone who can't speak, they won't answer you during the break when you ask them if they want a cup of tea. It's very disruptive and it's exhausting and it shows no respect for the team. Method acting is anathema to me. When I encounter it, I have to waste energy to protect myself from it.

Method actors are not team players.

Leading this group, with all his charm, intelligence, and good looks, is the three-time Oscar winner Daniel Day-Lewis. In the beginning of filming *My Left Foot*, knowing little about method acting, I used to go to the canteen with him to help him eat, staying in character as his mother. His character, Christy Brown, couldn't speak, so Daniel wouldn't speak, which somewhat limited the conversation.

Next day, we were in the canteen again. This time I decided to chat away and that he could nod his head in response.

Next day, knowing that everyone else was up in the bar having a good time, I said, 'Fuck this,' and went straight in with some hard questions, like: 'When you were playing the dentist in *Eversmile*, did you have to learn how to pull people's teeth out?' 'Uh, uh,' he grunted. Next day: 'When you were preparing for *Gandhi*, did you have to go around punching Indians in the face?' 'Ugh, ugh, ugh,' he said, showing some irritation. Next day: 'When you were in *My Beautiful Launderette*, did you bugger some lad to know what it was like to be homosexual?'

This time it got him and I smiled to myself as he grunted loudly and then told me to fuck off.

And so I did, joining the rest of cast in the bar and leaving him alone with his method.

Barry, Divorce

I can breathe because I know nothing is touching me. I can breathe because I can't feel.

A slant of shade touched his cheek and, in a moment, I loved all of him again.

Me. The slag. The slag he didn't know. Should I have shown her? Would he have liked her? But then who'd have dug the pit?

He hadn't drunk the dirt or dipped his hands into my damaged heart to find it empty.

I knew that he could bruise me. Not by anything he'd do, but by his imagination. His cleverness.

There were still things I felt he *could* do to me, thought he *might* do to me.

But then, of course, there is the one thing.

The one thing that he

… *did* do to me.

Brenda's husband Barry picking her poppies.

Bogarde

Cassie phoned me at one minute past noon, which made me smile. Having been born an owl, and having made many friends who were larks, and knowing larks were a selfish lot, not thinking twice about phoning me at the crack of dawn, I would have to become serious about it to the point of dropping a couple of friends.

But Cassie who is – as they say – A Classy Lady, always respected my request to be left alone in the morning, adding humour to it by phoning me dead on the last bong of the midday church bells close to her. I was so very fond of Cassie. She was kind and gentle – until, that is, she was drawing up a contract for a client.

'There's a book called *Utz* written by a man called Bruce Chatwin,' she said and asked me if I'd read it.

I said, no, but I'd heard of it.

'Same here. You go out and buy it. I'll do the same. We can both read it, and then and talk about it. A director called George Sluizer is making a film of it and he's interested in you for the part of Marta.'

'Okay,' I said, and within twenty minutes I was at the station waiting for a Tube to take me to Leicester Square. The Tube never ceased to thrill me. It was like being at the carnival and driving into spooky tunnels. Going underground felt like an arrow being shot from a bow, and of course the speed of getting from outer London straight through to Central London was amazing.

I walked along Charing Cross Road. My stomach was in knots with anticipation, as I approached one of the most exciting bookshops in the world. Foyles. My friend Kate Binchy had introduced me to it a few years before and it had instantly become a major part of my life.

Both my father and Barry had used libraries, but I went for bookshops, partly because of my addiction to the feel and smell of the paper. I took a deep breath before stepping through into the enchanted caves filled to the brim with books. My heart missed a beat as I approached a staff member to ask for *Utz*. She didn't give me time to name the author but turned fast on her dangerously high-heeled shoes and marched down one of the long aisles, stopping midway and spreading her arms, saying, 'Here's a selection of Bruce Chatwin books.' And then she was gone. Thank goodness I wasn't in a hurry, as when I remembered to check my watch I saw that two and a half hours had gone in a second.

I left with four books. It would have been ten but for my budget. I paid at the till and watched my books being carefully placed into a beautiful dark green paper bag with one word on it written in gold letters: FOYLES. I strolled back down Charing Cross Road, relaxed and with a smile, maybe a smirk, as I swung my carrier bag back and forth, unashamedly happy.

I got home delighted with myself and buzzing from my Foyles fix. I wasn't able to read on the Tube as the evening rush had well started. Almost everyone I knew complained about this, but I loved being pushed up against every kind of human imaginable. Quite often I would wiggle my way to get close to a Black man. Black skin was so beautiful to me. Some of the men had skin like a baby's bum, eyelashes Kate

Moss would kill for. The whites of their eyes were as white as snow, making their beautiful brown eyes even more so. Not a blemish in sight. Thinking back on it now, I blush. How many dark-skinned men did I make feel uncomfortable by openly staring?

I ran up the stairs and got into bed. I always read in bed. It was something I was much mocked for. The arrogance of well-educated people has never failed to amaze me. It still does.

I went downstairs again, took the phone off the hook, went back upstairs, got back into the bed, curled up, and read Mr Chatwin's book. As always, when reading a good book, time flew by, and it was midnight by the time I phoned Cassie. Her answering machine was on so I left a simple message telling her that it was a marvellous book, that it had great filmic potential, and that I was keen to hear what she thought. I went back to bed knowing I would sleep the sleep that only reading a good book can give you.

The next day we agreed to meet at a pub for lunch. As always, I was early. Hard slaps from Bina had taught me that. When Cassie arrived I was, as always, surprised at how young she looked. A wise, cool head on young shoulders. I stood up to greet her, gave her a warm hug, and asked her what she wanted to drink.

'A glass of house white wine, please,' she answered in her posh English accent.

I had ordered a pint of Guinness, and the drinks arrived ten minutes later. While I scowled at the badly pulled pint, Cassie quietly ordered a salad sandwich. She was chattering away about some news item of the day and I grew impatient to hear what she had to say.

'For God's sake, Cassie, would ya stop torturing me?' I said.

She threw her head back and laughed that dark, sexy laugh of hers. 'Okay, okay. So be prepared, Brenda.'

'C'mon, c'mon,' I said impatiently as she delicately touched her lips with a paper serviette. 'For God's sake, Cassie, stop teasing me!'

She quietly folded her hands on the table, then, from nowhere, she let out a sort of gasp before leaning across the table and whispering in my ear, 'Okay, okay. Now, firstly, one of your favourite actors will be playing the lead.'

'Who? C'mon, tell me, who?'

'Well, he's only agreed to do it, he hasn't signed the contract yet.'

'Okay, Cassie, c'mon, stop teasing me?'

She took a deep breath before whispering quietly in her cut-glass tones, speaking straight into my eyes: *'DIRK BOGARDE!!!* Yes, yes! Dirk Bogarde!'

I could barely breathe. I couldn't speak. I felt a rush of blood to my face.

'What, what?' she cried.

'THE Dirk Bogarde?' I asked, as if there were two.

'Yes, Brenda. THE Dirk Bogarde.'

'Aaah, Cassie, stop that. Stop. That's cruel. Don't tease me. Because I know for a fact that he is well retired, and living the good life in France, and refusing all offers of work from everybody.'

'Uh-uh.'

She shook her head, wagging her finger in my face

I saw the twinkle in her eye and I knew she was telling the truth. Completely losing my composure now, 'DIRK BOGARDE!' I shouted. Jumping out of my seat I grabbed her neck and kissed her head, frightening all the men sitting at the bar.

Fuck, I thought as I ran wildly to the men at the counter and breathed heavily into their faces, *I'm about to meet one of my lifetime heroes in the flesh AND I'm going to work with him.*

'How about that?' I repeated, screaming madly at the ceiling. 'Yes! Yes! Yes!'

My shouting caused a bit of a reaction. I felt Cassie's hand on my shoulder. Through her own laugh she was saying, 'Sit down, Brenda. Sit down, for goodness' sake. Sit down.'

'Drinks for everyone in the house!' I shouted out. Then, quite dramatically, I downed the remaining half pint in one gulp and the men at the bar laughed happily and freely as they watched me smacking my lips in delight. I turned around to Cassie and kissed her fiercely on the mouth, and she cried out, 'Stop, stop, Brenda! Sit down for goodness' sake ...' But I shouted for another pint before falling back into my chair and smiling from ear to ear.

Sitting down, I realized I was shaking from head to toe.

'Are you all right?' she asked. And then without warning, I started crying. I leaned my arms on the table, then leaned my head on my arms, exhaustion, disbelief, and delight flooding through me. Out of the corner of my eye I saw Cassie gently smiling as she neatly bit off a corner of her salad sandwich, rather enjoying the excitement surrounding her.

Three hours later, I packed and unpacked my suitcase, such as it was. A battered old thing well-worn from scores of trips back and forth on the Holyhead ferry. Suddenly I blushed, feeling as though Dirk Bogarde could see me. I threw it onto the floor, went back down to the car, and drove to Ealing Green, where there was a small sports shop. I saw a neat little black suitcase in the window. I ran in and bought it and was back in the house within thirty minutes. Ten minutes later I was packing.

Within forty-eight hours I was at the airport. A beautiful summer's day. I got through Heathrow airport surprisingly quickly and once on the plane I read the script over and over and over again, all the way to Prague. I had the book, too, which, barely a novella, I was able to read again on the flight. I had done more research than I usually did. I had read about how Mr Bogarde prepared for a film, and then Cassie had phoned again to tell me that Mr Paul Scofield was playing the bookshop owner.

Excitement is exhausting, so I was knackered when I arrived. At Prague airport, I got through quite quickly, and I spotted the man holding up a card with my name on it. I handed him my little suitcase and then settled back into a very plush seat in a very plush car. Creature comforts everyone should have every day of their lives. After about twenty-five minutes of driving through quite dull countryside we arrived at the edge of the city, where I saw elegant, ornate baroque architecture. We pulled up outside a small, white, dull modern building. It crossed my mind that this might not be quite the oasis of luxury I had heard other actors talking about. But who the fuck cared? Dirky was in there!

Calm down, Brenda, calm down. This is just another actor and another job.

The foyer was completely empty, so I checked in, got a key, and then followed a child in a uniform to room 148, in a hotel in a city where I was to work for the next five weeks with two of the greatest actors of our time, and with a director I had been told by reliable sources was very good indeed.

I was shown to my room. It was small, and had an annex with a small TV. I unpacked my small case, putting the few clothes I had brought onto the clothes hangers and putting my knickers into the drawers. Travelling light was good. What with working ten to twelve hours a day, wearing a well-thought-out costume, you'd only spend five or six hours in your personal clothes.

I went straight to the phone and ordered up a pint of Guinness. I washed my hands and face and dried them on a fluffy, maroon-coloured towel. I prowled the room checking out the windows, the wardrobe, the bedside table, and the desk. The desk was unashamedly old and unashamedly beautiful, gorgeous with shiny, maroon-coloured hotel paper, pens, and envelopes.

I undressed and lay on the heavy linen sheets, script in hand, ready to read it again.

Surprised at how tired I was, I fell into a light sleep, from which I was awoken by a gentlemanly knock on the door. I opened it to see an extremely handsome young man with a tray in his hands and my perfectly poured Guinness on the tray. I ushered him in and he sashayed across the room to the small table and placed it down carefully, showing due respect. Smiling to myself, I reached into my jeans and pulled out what I had been told was the equivalent of a fiver, which he gracefully plucked from my hand before sashaying back out.

I picked up the pint and went over to the window to see the view. I remembered that the director, George Sluizer, had said he'd phone at eight or thereabouts, so as it was only five o'clock, I had two or three more pints and felt very, very good indeed. At eight on the dot the phone rang and, true to his word, it was George Sluizer. He was stuck in a meeting, he explained, and it would be nine or nine thirty before he'd get to me, but not to worry he'd booked a table at the U Medvídků where we'd have a fabulous meal and a wonderful night.

George called from the foyer at quarter past nine, asking if he could he come up to meet me and welcome me to Prague. He turned out to be neither big nor tall nor wide nor thin. What he did have was a big, beaming smile that showed off a set of godly white teeth. With a flash of envy I threw my arms around him, saying how wonderful it was to meet him. He grinned from ear to ear, observing my drink and, ever so suavely, ordered the same again from the hovering porter. George asked if I was okay. How was the flight? he queried. Any trouble getting through security? How did I feel about being there? Did the driver look after me? What was my first impression of Prague? He made all these mundane questions seem like outrageous compliments. Oh, the charm and confidence of sophisticated men never fails to impress me. I instantly liked him. He was a naturally elegant man with a grey and white beard, brown-red curly hair, and sparkling blue eyes. When he spoke, his voice was warm but his tone made it quite clear he didn't suffer fools gladly. He overpowered me a little, but I have learned to ignore that feeling when there's humour in the mix, and he had a bottle of wine under his oxter.

I knew that the part I was going to play in the film was difficult. I would never call a part easy, in fact. I found them all difficult – sometimes very difficult – but with every line I needed a director's help. I had worked with young directors who went on to make it big – one was even knighted. When the BBC still had its *Play for Today* slot, I worked with fine directors like the brilliant Donald McWhinnie a few times. If you've had that privilege and survived it, you can work with any director.

Mr Sluizer held his bottle up, pointing at the label. Knowing absolutely nothing about wine, I feigned amazement, saying, 'Where did you manage to get that, Mr Sluizer?'

'It's from my private collection,' he said, 'and you can have some whenever you like.'

It was easy to slip a bottle of beautiful wine down as we went through the script page by page. After about an hour of this and after four or five glasses of excellent wine I was already feeling that here was a director who would be very good to work with. I loved his sense of humour. I loved how he helped, not hindered, me across some of the more obscure parts that I didn't fully understand. Relaxed and happy, I couldn't contain my excitement any longer. In a fake cool tone, I asked, 'Has Mr Scofield arrived yet? I'm his greatest fan.'

He laughed, saying that Mr Scofield was booked in and would be staying in the room next to mine.

I had a thousand questions to ask him about Paul and Dirk. Could I call him that? I wondered. I noticed my hands trembling slightly as I turned over pages of script. I had a few wonderful scenes with Mr Scofield. Now there was another form of terror. Mr Scofield was at the top of his professional game. He had graciously refused a knighthood, had played Thomas More in *A Man for All Seasons*, a film I had seen fourteen times, beaten only by *Jailhouse Rock*, in which I had seen Mr Elvis Presley fifteen times. Neither man had made a single mistake in either film: Elvis in his singing, and Mr Scofield in his acting. His breathing, his pauses, his stresses, his tones, his artistry guided us along a journey so delicately balanced, so full of glory and truth, indignation and sorrow, that come his execution at the end the dignity and peace he showed gave us just one fierce flash of fear; the dignity with which Thomas died – and Paul acted this – led to Scofield picking up all the prizes available to him that year.

Paul Scofield and Dirk Bogarde were internationally acclaimed and adored. These were the kind of actors I had learned from.

Several drinks later, George suggested we eat at the hotel rather than break the excellent mood and move to the restaurant. Happily, I agreed, saying I had had a sandwich on the plane. He suggested I have my first taste of Czech food right now. Eagerly agreeing, I watched him order, without a glance at the menu, cabbage pancakes for two with all the trimmings. Pausing for effect, he asked quietly for a bottle of Maison Trimbach with two cooled wine glasses. Appreciating the drama of it all, I burst out laughing, feeling as happy as I possibly could be, being wined and dined by this handsome, utterly charming director with whom I was about to start working in a day or two alongside two of the best actors of their generation. I was over-excited, over-enchanted, over-eager.

We talked awkwardly about the script, and I was thrilled by his bright, perceptive answers.

Knowing how well it was going, I turned to a piece of advice Barry had given me years before, which had stood me in good stead since: ask questions of the director. Actors don't do it nearly enough. Ask questions pertinent to the director's problems. Ask about the crew. Were there any problems getting the people he wanted? Were all his main actors easily available? What about locations?

'Use humour, Brenda,' Barry had advised. 'Always let a director know you have a sense of humour.'

So I asked George, 'Seeing how passionate you are about food, have you got the caterers sorted out yet?'

'Yes, yes, yes,' he gasped. 'Yes, yes, yes. Vital, isn't it?'

'Did you get all the actors you wanted? As we both know, that's the crucial one.'

'It is,' he replied softly. 'It is.'

With those two words, the atmosphere in the room changed.

'Yes, yes,' he said. 'It is vital.'

'What's wrong?' I asked. Had he made a mistake? About me? About casting me? Was that it?

He shrugged, as if to signify nothing, all was well.

Jesus, I thought, *I'd better get stuck in here, more stuck in. After all, I'll have Paul Scofield and Dirk Bogarde to discuss all this with.*

As I pushed these feeble, funky little thoughts towards his superior brain I just made myself sound stupider and stupider.

I changed tack.

'How wonderful!' I squeaked, feeling every ounce of blood in my body rush to my face. For a second I thought I might faint, but I just chirruped enthusiastically.

'Yes,' he said. 'Paul is resting. But we're all going to meet later and I'll take you out to one of the bars.'

I was suddenly exhausted from the months of waiting for this moment. Tired and unable to be quiet any longer I blurted out, 'And is Mr Bogarde in the hotel too? Has he arrived yet?'

Suddenly, George looked awful. What I had seen as beautiful hair was, I could see now, thin and pale. His hands were a little grubby. His teeth not white at all.

'Ah well, now ... about Mr Bogarde,' he sighed threateningly to himself.

'He's not sick, is he?' I heard myself quietly ask. 'Is he unwell? Something's gone wrong, I can sense it.'

Like most actors, my senses were good.

'Yes.' He sighed. 'There's been a big change. Well,' he gasped, 'you've been told that Mr Scofield is here.'

'Yes, yes! What, what, George?' I cried.

'Well, I'm afraid I've got bad news about Mr Bogarde.'

'What?' I whispered. 'What?' I asked again, knowing in my heart in that moment that something awful had happened.

'Well, I'm afraid Mr Bogarde changed his mind a few days ago.'

Stunned now. Completely stunned.

'What?' I said. 'Where is he? Where is he, George? Stop fooling, now. Where is he?' I spat into his face. 'Is he sick? What the fuck is going on?'

'No, no, no, Brenda, my dear, he changed his mind about doing the film.'

'WHAT?'

'He's changed his mind. Withdrawn. He's not coming. He won't be here. He's not doing the film. He phoned me two days ago to tell me he'd decided to withdraw from the film. Brenda, Brenda, it's not just you, my love. *Everyone* is gutted. We can't believe that he won't be in it. We're devastated.'

Feeling bile fill my mouth, something rattled there. A crash. A loud bang. My glass fell from my hand, my hand went to my face, my face folded in grief and my body fell to the floor. I cut my hand as I fell from the chair, I hit the floor mumbling the word '*Withdrawing?*' My stomach turned and a spoonful of vomit filled my mouth. I spat it out, all pretence at dignity gone.

'Yes, Brenda,' he said angrily, 'he's fucking withdrawn. Phoned me a few days ago. We're all distraught. I'm so sorry. I know how excited you were when you heard he was in it.'

I felt tears run down my face as I leaned over towards the friendly floor. George spoke gently as he lifted me back up. He put his arms around me and I fell into them shaking, near hysteria now. He held me very tight into him and I was grateful for that.

I don't know how long I cried on his shoulder. I just remember waking up, remembering, crying. He was no longer there.

George had left a note to see how I was. I felt ill. Had I thrown up? Yes. A bit of Aer Lingus sandwich was on the floor. I ordered a large vodka from room service and turned the TV on. The vodka came. I drank it. Ordered more. Drank that, and ordered more. Told the waiter to bring a bottle up. He did. I had another drink. The Coca-Cola tasted wrong. It was some kind of cheap drink, but it'd do.

An orchestra came on the telly. Beethoven. Sixth Symphony in F, I think. It was the signature tune for Des's radio show, *Down the Country with Fred Desmond*. His pseudonym. A pang of love and loneliness split me into two. I fell into the bed and cried again. Tears of utter loss. I drifted off and woke up again. Poured another drink. The room was so hot. It was summertime and the heating was too high. The radiator seemed stuck. I phoned down for help to be told again that this was the temperature the hotel had all year round: 'It's part of the health scheme.' Health scheme? Eh? 'Yes, this is Prague's leading Health Hotel!'

I phoned George and sniffled my complaint to him, to which he answered, 'Oh, yeah, it's a Health Hotel. Low heat in all the building all year round. It's amazing.'

'No, it isn't,' I answered sharply. 'There's sweat dripping out of every pore!'

Was I slurring my words? What the fuck?

'Well, it's awful here,' I persisted. 'Get me into another hotel NOW!'

'Brenda,' he said gently, 'it's two thirty in the morning. I'll deal with this tomorrow. Go to bed now.'

I was furious – proper anger – at the whole thing.

Well, I thought, *if Mr Bogarde thinks he can get away with this ... fuck him. Fuck the film.*

I just wanted my own bed. I picked up the phone to call George again, remembering last minute it was the middle of the night. I put the phone down. I lost my balance. Felt my clothes sticking to my sweaty skin. I ran to the bathroom, ripped them off and ran a cold bath. I gasped as my body voluntarily sat down into the glorious coolness. Almost fainting now from the heat I emptied the bath, turned the cold tap on again, filled the bath again, dunked my head under it again. Nothing was working. *Think, Brenda.*

I got out of the bath, went to the bed, pulled off the sheets, ran back, drenched them in cold water, ran back to let them dribble. I didn't wring them. Went back to the bed, lay down, and pulled the cold, wet sheet right up over my body until I was completely encased in it, from head to toe. I was rewarded with a twenty-second taste of heaven. My body cooled but then heated up again.

As disappointment turned to rage I dragged myself over to the little desk and the elegant hotel stationery. I sat quietly down, picked up a biro from the pen holder, and in a mood as cold as ice I began my letter:

Dear Mr Fucking Bogarde! How dare you pull out of this film? You're an unprofessional cunt and if ever I meet you – something I've wanted to do for years – I certainly won't shake your bloody hand. I'll spit at you instead.

I actually posted that letter from Prague; I sent it to Cassie to send to Dirk's agent, who would give it to him. The minute it had fallen into the letterbox I regretted it. I tried to contact Cassie, but she had gone away, and a young girl in her office took it upon herself to send it to Dirk.

He didn't answer straight away, but when the filming was over, I got an answer, half hand-written, half-typed. He was gracious, saying that everything I had said was true, and that he was glad I hadn't held back about his behaviour, letting everybody down a week before the film was supposed to start. We were pen pals for years after that. We became friends.

Brenda and Richard Harris during the filming of *The Field*.

Becoming Invisible

Becoming invisible. That's what Richard Harris and I talked about, sitting in the rain on the rocks looking out over the Atlantic Ocean on that day, all those years ago. One as curious as the other about the words he'd just uttered. About becoming invisible at the age of seventy. We were surprised that we were so together in the strength of our curiosity. Oh, how eager he was to walk every inch of that last mile of life. I felt it with him, but then death came early to him. He would have laughed, called out the odds, and wished me better luck than him.

I bumped into him on a flight to Belgium months before he died. He was seated up at the front, me way down the back. He spotted me and sprinted like a schoolboy down the aisle, fell onto his knees, bringing that famous face close to mine. But he looked dreadful, absolutely dreadful, and he knew it. He nudged my shoulder, whispering loudly and excitedly in that Limerick accent: 'Fricker! D'ya rimimber? Do ya? D'ya rimimber the rocks, Brinda? D'ya rimimber our talk on the rocks? D'ya remember that day, Brinda?'

I put my arm around his shoulder. Fearing the bones might break, I whispered, 'Yes, I do, Richard. I remember every word, every silence, every breath.'

He beamed in pleasure or in pain as I kissed his withered cheek. He stood up awkwardly and walked slowly back up the aisle, but the walk was laboured. That bony back was bent, his hand swiping at that lone, long lank grey hair.

And now I have a ghost beside me. An empty rock to balance me. I will not have that space filled with kind people doing kind things to please themselves.

But now, today, this minute, when I'm in this place alone, I find I'm weak. My vision's blurred. My body's beat.

My heart is strong. It's fit to fight. But no one knows. Not one person. Can I do this alone? The way I have planned? Alone?

I'm stifling myself with effort in the wrong direction.

Stop.

Work.

Breathe.

Prepare to take this first last step.

The Prize

What I wasn't aware of in the early days was that further down the line my whole life would be turned upside down. That I would be brought to the far side of the world, into a new world I never knew was real. That I would be led into a dreamland full of shiny folk, of blinding lights, where strangers full of dreamy words would hang a prize around my neck, a dazzling golden prize that said I was the *best in all the world*. That shouted out, 'She gets The Prize! She is the best!' And there I was for just a beat – for just one single beat – I fell for all of it! I felt the glow. I drank it all, got drunk on all of it.

And there she was, my mother's face, sweet Bina's face. Her eyes were clear, her tears were clean, her pride was far too bright to bear. Her sorrow too was saying to me she never meant one blow of it. She never meant to cause me pain. She'd loved me all the time, she said. She knew I'd win that prize, she said. She'd loved me all the time, she said. *She'd loved me all the time*. She'd loved me all the time, she said.

I felt the lights, I heard the noise. Was that her heart in pieces now or was it mine or was it both, entwined at last? I heard the noise, I saw the stars, I said some words and walked into a world that would change the whole of me forever.

Acknowledgements

Thanks to Philip Belfield, Thom Fitzgerald, Tadhg O'Sullivan, Deirdre Nuttall, Virginia Gilbert, Max Edwards, Neil Belton, and Juno – without whose help, not one word of this book would ever have been written.

About the Author

BRENDA FRICKER (born 17 February 1945) is an Irish actress, whose career has spanned six decades on stage and screen. She has appeared in more than 30 films and television roles. In 1990, she became the first Irish actress to win an Academy Award, earning the award for Best Supporting Actress for the biopic *My Left Foot* (1989). She also appeared in films such as *The Field* (1990), *Home Alone 2: Lost in New York* (1992), *So I Married an Axe Murderer* (1993), *Angels in the Outfield* (1994), *A Time to Kill* (1996), *Veronica Guerin* (2003), *Inside I'm Dancing* (2004) and *Albert Nobbs* (2011).